MYSTICAL PLANTS IN DRUIDIC TRADITIONS

From Mistletoe to Oak: Understanding the Druidic Herbal Lexicon

D.R. T STEPHENS

S.D.N Publishing

CONTENTS

GENERAL DISCLAIMER

This book is intended to provide informative and educational material on the subject matter covered. The author(s), publisher, and any affiliated parties make no representations or warranties with respect to the accuracy, applicability, completeness, or suitability of the contents herein and specifically disclaim any implied warranties of merchantability or fitness for a particular purpose.

The information contained in this book is for general information purposes only and is not intended to serve as legal, medical, financial, or any other form of professional advice. Readers should consult with appropriate professionals before making any decisions based on the information provided. Neither the author(s) nor the publisher shall be held responsible or liable for any loss, damage, injury, claim, or otherwise, whether direct or indirect, consequential, or incidental, that may occur as a result of applying or misinterpreting the information in this book.

This book may contain references to third-party websites, products, or services. Such references do not constitute an endorsement or recommendation, and the author(s) and publisher are not responsible for any outcomes related to these third-party references.

In no event shall the author(s), publisher, or any affiliated parties be liable for any direct, indirect, punitive, special, incidental, or other consequential damages arising directly or indirectly from any use of this material, which is provided "as is," and without warranties of any kind, express or implied.

By reading this book, you acknowledge and agree that you assume all risks and responsibilities concerning the applicability and consequences of the information provided. You also agree to indemnify, defend, and hold harmless the author(s), publisher, and any affiliated parties from any and all liabilities, claims, demands, actions, and causes of action whatsoever, whether or not foreseeable, that may arise from using or misusing the information contained in this book.

Although every effort has been made to ensure the accuracy of the information in this book as of the date of publication, the landscape of the subject matter covered is continuously evolving. Therefore, the author(s) and publisher expressly disclaim responsibility for any errors or omissions and reserve the right to update, alter, or revise the content without prior notice.

By continuing to read this book, you agree to be bound by the terms and conditions stated in this disclaimer. If you do not agree with these terms, it is your responsibility to discontinue use of this book immediately.

CHAPTER 1: A WELCOMING FORAY INTO DRUIDIC HERBALISM

Welcome, dear reader, to a realm where nature whispers ancient secrets, and every leaf and twig holds a story. This is the verdant world of "Mystical Plants in Druidic Traditions: From Mistletoe to Oak: Understanding the Druidic Herbal Lexicon," a journey into the heart of the natural wisdom espoused by the Druids, the revered priestly class of the ancient Celts. Our exploration is not merely a botanical study; it is a voyage into the mystic, where flora intertwines with the spiritual and the mundane blossoms into the magical.

The Druids, often veiled in the mists of history, were the scholars, judges, and mediators between the physical and the ethereal realms. Their profound connection with nature was not only practical but also deeply spiritual. Plants were not merely resources but were imbued with sacred significance, integral to rituals, healing practices, and divination.

Before we delve into the verdant depths, let us first familiarize ourselves with the basic tenets of Druidic herbalism and why it captivates the modern mind.

The Essence of Druidic Herbalism

Druidic herbalism transcends the conventional boundaries of using plants for sustenance and medicine. For the Druids, plants were living, breathing entities, each possessing a unique spirit and consciousness. They were allies in healing, protectors in the spiritual realm, and guides in the pursuit of wisdom. The Druids believed in the interconnectedness of all life forms, and plants were a tangible manifestation of this intricate web of existence.

The Mistletoe and the Oak

The mystical allure of mistletoe, often referred to as the "All-Heal," captures the essence of Druidic reverence for plants. It was not harvested but rather "revered," with rituals dictating its collection. Similarly, the oak tree stood as a mighty symbol of strength, resilience, and wisdom. Its association with the god of thunder, the protective spirit of the tribe, and its use in various rites illustrate the depth of meaning attributed to plants in Druidic culture.

The Invitation

As we embark on this journey together, we invite you to suspend the cloak of modern skepticism and open your heart to the possibility of a world where plants are not mere silent spectators but sentient beings, communicating in a language that transcends words. Whether you are a botanist, a historian, a spiritual seeker, or simply a curious soul, there is something in this exploration for you. We begin with the basics, gradually peeling back the layers to reveal the intricate tapestry of Druidic herbalism.

As we progress from the introductory chapters to the intermediate discussions and finally to the advanced revelations, the complexity of language and concepts will evolve. Starting from the approachable and familiar, we will journey together into the realms of the profound and esoteric. Each chapter will build upon the last, crafting a comprehensive understanding of the Druidic herbal lexicon.

In the chapters to come, we will explore the historical Druids, the significance of various plants in their practices, and how these ancient traditions find relevance in our modern world. We will discover the sacred groves, the mystical properties of plants, and the intricate rituals that weave nature into the fabric of Druidic life. And as we journey through the intermediate and advanced levels, we will delve into the symbolic, metaphysical, and even quantum dimensions of Druidic plant lore.

We commence this expedition not as mere spectators but as active participants in an age-old dialogue between humans and the natural world. Our journey promises to be as enriching as it is enlightening, filled with wonder, wisdom, and perhaps a newfound appreciation for the green companions that grace our Earth.

Let us step forward with an open mind and a respectful heart, ready to uncover the secrets held within the leaves and branches of the mystical plants in Druidic traditions. Welcome to a world where every plant has a story, and every story is a thread in the tapestry of life. Welcome to the enchanting groves of Druidic herbalism.

CHAPTER 2: WHO WERE THE DRUIDS? A HISTORICAL OVERVIEW

Venturing deeper into the verdant realms of Druidic traditions, we must first acquaint ourselves with the enigmatic figures central to these practices: the Druids themselves. Emerging from the mists of history, Druids have long captivated the collective imagination, often depicted as wise sages, custodians of ancient lore, and intermediaries between the natural world and the realms beyond.

The Ancient Druids: Priests and Philosophers

The Druids were the esteemed religious leaders, legal authorities, lorekeepers, medical professionals, and political advisors of the Celtic tribes that once populated regions of what are now known as the British Isles and parts of Western Europe, particularly France. Their origins are shrouded in antiquity, with their influence believed to have flourished during the Iron Age, a period dating roughly from 800 BCE to 100 CE.

Despite the scarcity of written records from the Druids themselves, due to their oral tradition, we glean insight into their world through the writings of Roman historians, such as

Julius Caesar, and later, the medieval texts of Irish and Welsh origin. These sources, while admittedly external and sometimes skewed by cultural biases, nevertheless provide a tapestry of information, portraying Druids as a highly educated class undergoing rigorous training that could span over two decades, mastering a breadth of knowledge that encompassed theology, astronomy, philosophy, and the natural sciences.

The Sacred Role of Druids

Druids were considered intermediaries between the human realm and the supernatural world, conducting rituals, sacrifices, and ceremonies to ensure balance and harmony within their communities and the natural world. They were the caretakers of sacred spaces, such as the nemetons—groves of trees deemed as sanctuaries for worship and justice. Their adjudicative role was paramount, as they were the arbiters of disputes and the preservers of tribal customs and laws.

One of their most significant and enduring legacies is the Druidic calendar, a testament to their profound astronomical knowledge, encapsulating the seasonal cycles and celestial events. This calendar not only guided agricultural practices but also the timing of festivals and rituals, imbuing the rhythms of nature with cultural and spiritual significance.

Decline and Transformation

The influence of the Druids began to wane with the Roman conquest of Celtic lands, as the Romans, wary of their power and status, suppressed Druidic practices. Subsequent Christianization further relegated their traditions to the fringes of society. However, the Druidic legacy endured, morphing and integrating into the folklore and customs that persisted even as their religious prominence faded. The medieval texts, particularly those of Irish origin, continued to romanticize and eulogize the Druids, often casting them as enchanters and seers, thus ensuring their legacy would continue to intrigue and inspire for generations.

In conclusion, the Druids, as historical figures, are enigmatic and compelling, their true essence obscured by the veils of time. Yet, their reverence for nature, profound knowledge, and spiritual gravitas have left an indelible mark on the cultural and metaphysical landscapes of the regions they once inhabited. Their relationship with the natural world, particularly their veneration of plants and trees, forms the bedrock upon which we will build our exploration of the mystical plants in Druidic traditions in the subsequent chapters.

CHAPTER 3: PLANT LORE IN CELTIC MYTHOLOGY

In the verdant tapestry of Celtic mythology, plants are not mere background elements; they are vital threads woven intricately into the cultural and spiritual fabric of the Celtic people. This chapter delves into the mythic significance of plants within the Druidic tradition, elucidating their roles and symbolism in the rich tapestry of Celtic lore.

The Mythic Flora: An Enchanted Lexicon

In Celtic mythology, plants were not viewed as inanimate, passive entities but as living beings imbued with spirit and intention. This animistic perception infused the Celtic world with a sense of enchantment, where every plant held a story, a purpose, and a connection to the divine. The Druids, as the learned class among the Celts, were the custodians of this knowledge, understanding the language of the trees and herbs and conveying their wisdom to their communities.

One of the most emblematic plants in Celtic mythology is the oak tree. Revered as the king of trees, the oak was synonymous with strength, stability, and nobility. It was considered a cosmic storehouse of wisdom, its deep roots reaching into the underworld and its branches touching the heavens. Druids, whose very name is derived from the Celtic word for oak, "Duir," conducted their sacred ceremonies in oak groves, believing these spaces to be portals to other realms.

The ash tree held similar esteem, regarded as a cosmic axis that connected the three layers of the Celtic cosmos: the underworld, the earthly realm, and the heavens. Its wood was used to fashion spears and wands, tools believed to harness the tree's ability to bridge worlds.

In contrast to the towering presence of the oak and ash, the humble mistletoe held a more mystical allure. This parasitic plant, often found growing on oak trees, was thought to be the offspring of lightning striking the oak—a gift from the sky god. The Druids harvested it with great ceremony, capturing its essence to use in rites of fertility and healing.

Enchanted Groves and Sacred Blossoms

Celtic myths are replete with tales of enchanted groves and blossoms with magical properties. These stories served not only as entertainment but also as a means of imparting wisdom about the natural world and its connection to the divine.

One such tale is that of the Apple Branch of the Otherworld, a symbol of divine bounty and enlightenment. It is said that an apple branch from the Otherworld, bearing blossoms, fruit, and a sweet melody, was a ticket to the realm of eternal youth and beauty—a realm where time stood still, and sorrow was unknown.

Another tale speaks of the Hawthorn tree, also known as the fairy tree. It was believed that hawthorn groves were favorite gathering places for fairies, and to harm a hawthorn was to invite misfortune. Its blossoms were associated with the festival of Beltane, a time of fertility and the celebration of life.

The hazel tree was the bearer of wisdom. Its nuts, when eaten by the Salmon of Knowledge, were said to impart all the world's wisdom to the one who consumed the fish. Druids and poets sought the hazel for inspiration, drinking from the well of wisdom that lay beneath its branches.

Weaving the Mythic and the Mundane

For the Celts, the line between the mythic and the mundane was not a boundary but a spectrum. The stories of enchanted flora were not mere fairy tales but a means of understanding the world around them. These myths served as vehicles for imparting knowledge about the properties of plants, their uses, and their spiritual significance.

The Druids, as mediators between the natural world and the community, used these stories to teach about the cycles of nature, the interdependence of all living things, and the respect that must be accorded to the natural world. In doing so, they nurtured a culture that saw itself as part of a larger, living cosmos, where every plant, tree, and blade of grass held its own spirit and story.

As we conclude this exploration into the mythical flora of Celtic tradition, we are reminded that these stories, though ancient, carry timeless wisdom. They beckon us to look beyond the superficial and see the deeper connections that bind us to the natural world. In the next chapter, we shall step into the sacred groves of the Druids, where the tangible and the transcendent intertwine in the heart of nature.

CHAPTER 4: THE SACRED GROVES

In the verdant fabric of Druidic traditions, the sacred groves hold a distinguished and almost arcane significance. These natural sanctuaries, known as "nemeton" in the Druidic tongue, served not merely as places of worship or ceremonial congregation but as vibrant nexuses of the Druids' profound connection with nature. They were the bastions of biodiversity, spiritual resonance, and ecological wisdom. By delving into the composition and sacredness of these groves, one can begin to appreciate their quintessential role in Druidic practices.

The Essence of Sacred Groves

The groves were more than mere clusters of trees; they were seen as portals to the otherworld, teeming with a vitality that transcended the physical realm. Each tree, shrub, and blade of grass was infused with spirit, contributing to the grove's collective sanctity. The Druids believed that these spaces were alive with the whispers of their ancestors, the breath of the earth, and the very essence of the cosmos. It was here that the veil between the worlds was perceived as thinnest, enabling profound spiritual interactions and divine revelations.

Common Trees in Druidic Groves

The composition of sacred groves was no random assortment of flora; it was a deliberate congregation of specific trees, each holding profound significance within the Druidic belief system.

- **Oak (Quercus robur):** The oak tree, with its robust trunk and far-reaching branches, symbolized strength, endurance, and wisdom. It was considered the king of the grove, often serving as the central axis around which other trees were arranged. Its association with the god Dagda and the lightning-bearer Taranis imbued it with divine connotations.

- **Ash (Fraxinus excelsior):** Representing the world axis or the "Yggdrasil" in Norse cosmology, the ash tree held a place of respect in Druidic groves. It symbolized connection, harmony, and the balance between the upper, middle, and lower realms.

- **Hawthorn (Crataegus monogyna):** Often associated with the realm of faeries and the festival of Beltane, the hawthorn was a symbol of fertility and protection. Its blossoms were considered especially potent and were used in various rites and rituals.

- **Birch (Betula pendula):** Representing new beginnings and purification, the birch tree was often found at the periphery of sacred groves. Its presence was believed to ward off negative energies and facilitate a rejuvenation of the spirit.

- **Yew (Taxus baccata):** The yew tree, with its longevity and evergreen nature, was a potent symbol of death, rebirth, and eternity. Often found in burial grounds, it reminded the Druids of the cyclical nature of existence and the persistence of the soul.

The Spiritual Function of Groves

The groves were the Druids' temples, libraries, and universities, all interwoven into the living tapestry of the forest. Here, under the dappled light of the canopy, the Druids conducted their most sacred rituals, including initiations, seasonal festivals, and rites of passage. The groves served as classrooms where knowledge was passed from one generation to the next, not through written texts but through oral traditions, symbolism, and direct communion with nature.

Divination, a cornerstone of Druidic practice, was also conducted within the sacred confines of the grove. The whispering leaves, the patterns of birds in flight, and the rustling wildlife all served as mediums through which divine messages were interpreted. The groves were not just places for seeking guidance for the future but also sanctuaries for healing, reflection, and deep meditation.

In essence, Chapter 4 unravels the deep-seated reverence Druids held for their sacred groves. These groves were not just physical spaces but profound spiritual landscapes that mirrored the cosmos in their complexity and beauty. They were the living temples where every tree, every stone, and every brook was imbued with sacredness and served as a testament to the Druids' veneration for the natural world. The groves remind us that in the heart of nature lies a profound wisdom and a timeless spirituality that continues to echo through the ages.

CHAPTER 5: MISTLETOE: THE GOLDEN BOUGH

Mistletoe, the enigmatic plant often associated with festive kissing, holds a far more profound significance within the annals of Druidic tradition. This peculiar plant, neither tree nor shrub, was exalted by the Druids and shrouded in a mystique that transcended mere decoration. Known in the ancient Celtic language as "All Heal," mistletoe was revered as a powerful emblem of vitality, fertility, and an arbiter of peace.

The Enchantment of Mistletoe

Mistletoe is a hemiparasitic plant, which means it partially relies on its host, typically an oak or apple tree, for sustenance. Its curious nature, sprouting from the branches of mighty trees, imbued it with a sense of magic in the Druidic worldview. The fact that it remained green even during the frigid winter months only heightened its mystical status. It seemed to defy the laws of nature, surviving and thriving when all around it succumbed to the frost's embrace.

The Druids perceived the mistletoe as a celestial gift, a botanical marvel birthed not from the earth but from the heavens. This belief stemmed from its unusual propagation method; mistletoe seeds are often spread by birds, and the Druids considered birds as messengers from the divine realms. Hence, mistletoe was deemed a sacred bridge between the celestial and terrestrial planes, a verdant jewel bestowed by the gods.

The Ritual of the Oak and Mistletoe

The most significant and enigmatic Druidic ceremony involving mistletoe was the ritual of the Oak and Mistletoe. This ceremony was typically conducted during the sixth day of the moon's cycle, a period the Druids believed to be most auspicious. The chosen oak, seen as the king of the forest, would be sought out – its branches scrutinized for the presence of the sacred plant.

Upon discovering a mistletoe-laden oak, the Druids would prepare for a ritual of harvesting, a ceremonial act imbued with solemn reverence and intricate symbolism. A Druid clad in white robes, symbolizing purity and the celestial origin of mistletoe, would ascend the oak. With a golden sickle, a tool reflective of the sun and its life-giving radiance, the Druid would carefully sever the mistletoe from its arboreal cradle. Below, fellow Druids would hold a cloth to catch the plant, ensuring it never touched the earth and preserved its divine essence.

This harvested mistletoe was considered an elixir of life, a potent remedy against poison, and a talisman to ensure fertility and protect against malevolent forces. The ceremony was not merely an act of gathering but a profound communion with the divine, a harmonization of humanity with the sacred rhythms of nature.

Mistletoe in Medicine and Myth

Beyond its ceremonial use, mistletoe held a prominent place in Druidic medicine. It was prescribed for a plethora of ailments, ranging from epilepsy to hypertension. Its purported healing powers were so renowned that it was often referred to as "All

Heal," a panacea for the ills that beset both body and spirit.

Mythologically, mistletoe was interwoven with tales of resurrection and immortality. One such legend speaks of a god being slain with a weapon forged of mistletoe, only to be resurrected by the same plant. This narrative reinforced the Druidic belief in the cyclical nature of life, death, and rebirth, with mistletoe serving as a botanical symbol of eternal renewal.

A Symbol of Peace and Reconciliation

The mistletoe also occupied a significant role as a symbol of peace and reconciliation. Druidic lore tells of warring chieftains who would lay down their arms beneath a mistletoe-adorned oak, the sacred plant serving as a mediator for truce and harmony. This tradition persisted into the modern era, transmuted into the custom of kissing under the mistletoe, a gesture of goodwill and affection.

In essence, mistletoe, the Golden Bough of Druidic tradition, was not merely a plant but a multifaceted symbol interlacing themes of vitality, divinity, healing, and peace. Its peculiar biology and distinctive place in ritual and myth rendered it a botanical enigma, an emblem of the mystical synergy between humanity and the natural world. As we delve further into the verdant tapestry of Druidic plant lore, the mistletoe serves as a reminder of the profound reverence our ancestors held for the living world, a sentiment that remains ever relevant in our contemporary pursuit of harmony with nature.

CHAPTER 6: THE MIGHTY OAK AND THE DRUIDS

The oak tree, robust and enduring, has woven its way through the tapestry of time, embedding itself in the annals of Druidic traditions. Its stature in Druidism is not merely a consequence of its physical grandeur but also its embodiment of ancient wisdom and spiritual strength. This chapter delves into the intricate relationship between the mighty oak and the Druids, elucidating the symbolic and ceremonial significance it held within their practices.

The Oak: A Pillar of Druidic Beliefs

To comprehend the oak's esteemed position in Druidic lore, one must first appreciate the Druids' profound reverence for nature. They perceived trees not as inanimate entities but as living embodiments of the divine, each species whispering its unique wisdom to those attuned to listen. Among these sylvan oracles, the oak stood as the chieftain, a revered elder in the arboreal community.

The oak's longevity and resilience were perceived as a mirror to the Druids' quest for eternal knowledge and strength. Its expansive canopy was seen as a cosmic antenna, bridging the earthly realm with the celestial domains. Furthermore, the

Druids believed that the oak possessed a dense, vital energy — a kind of spiritual fortitude that could be harnessed during rituals and ceremonies. It's no surprise that groves of oak trees, known as "nemeton," were considered sacred spaces where the veil between worlds was thinnest.

Ceremonial Majesty: The Oak in Druidic Rites

Druidic rituals often took place in the embrace of these mighty oaks, where the Druids performed various ceremonies to mark the turning of the seasons, celebrate significant life events, and seek divine guidance. The summer solstice, a time of maximum daylight, was one such occasion when the oak's vitality was at its peak. Druids would gather under its boughs to pay homage to the sun, often using oak wood to fuel the ritual bonfires that symbolized life's renewal.

The oak was also central to one of the most enigmatic Druidic rituals — the harvesting of mistletoe. Mistletoe, which occasionally adorned the oak's branches, was considered a powerful and sacred plant. Its collection was a ceremonial affair, undertaken with great reverence and typically performed with a golden sickle, indicative of the ritual's significance. The oak's association with the mistletoe further augmented its mystical status, intertwining the fates of both plant and tree in Druidic cosmology.

Druidic Lore: The Oak's Symbolic Roots

In the rich tapestry of Druidic symbols, the oak held multiple meanings, each layer revealing deeper insights into the Druids' worldview. Its towering presence was symbolic of strength and stability, characteristics highly valued by the Druids. Furthermore, the oak's expansive root system, delving deep into the earth, was emblematic of grounding and connection to the land, reminding the Druids of the importance of a solid foundation in both spiritual and physical realms.

The oak's acorns, too, held special significance. They were seen as seeds of potential, embodying the promise of new beginnings and the perpetuation of life. Druids often used acorns in divination practices, seeking wisdom from their patterns and placements. In a broader sense, the acorns were a reminder of the cycle of life, death, and rebirth — a cycle deeply revered and celebrated in Druidic traditions.

In Summary

The oak tree, with its imposing stature and enduring nature, occupied a central place in the heart of Druidic practices. It was not only a symbol of strength, wisdom, and stability but also a sacred space where the Druids conducted their most profound rituals. Its role in Druidism is a testament to the profound connection the Druids felt with the natural world — a relationship built on reverence, symbiosis, and an understanding of the deep interweaving of all life. As we continue to explore the mystical plants in Druidic traditions, the oak stands as a majestic reminder of the ancient wisdom that once flourished under its boughs.

CHAPTER 7: ROWAN: THE WITCHWOOD

In the pantheon of Druidic flora, the Rowan tree holds a distinguished place, revered for its mystical attributes and protective essence. Known colloquially as the Witchwood, the Rowan tree, with its robust presence and fiery red berries, has woven itself into the fabric of Druidic beliefs, imbuing landscapes with a sense of the sacred. This chapter delves into the Rowan's revered position in Druidic tradition, exploring its symbolic significance, protective properties, and its role in rituals and mythology.

Symbolic Significance of Rowan

In the Druidic herbal lexicon, the Rowan tree is not just a plant but a symbol—a microcosm of the universe manifest in botanical form. Its place in Druidic tradition is both complex and profound, intertwining with themes of protection, vision, and gateway to the otherworld. The Rowan tree is often seen as a sentinel, guarding against malevolent forces with its fiery berries that blaze like beacons against the verdant foliage. The leaves of the Rowan, with their intricate, feather-like patterns, are said to represent the intricate tapestry of the cosmos, mirroring the interwoven threads of fate and destiny.

Protective Properties of Rowan

Druidic tradition imbues the Rowan tree with powerful protective properties, casting it as a shield against enchantments and ill fortune. It was common practice for Druids to carry talismans fashioned from Rowan wood or to plant the trees near dwellings and sacred sites. The Rowan's potency was believed to stem from the five-pointed stars, or pentagrams, found on the base of its berries. The pentagram, a symbol of protection and balance in many esoteric traditions, amplifies the Rowan's defensive properties, creating an invisible barrier against negative energies.

Rowan in Rituals and Mythology

The Rowan tree's integration into Druidic rituals underscores its spiritual importance. Branches laden with red berries were used in ceremonies to bless and protect, while its wood served as material for crafting wands and staffs, tools integral to the channeling of energy. In the realm of mythology, the Rowan frequently features as a bridge to the otherworld, its branches a ladder between realms, enabling communication with spirits and ancestors. This otherworldly connection positions the Rowan as a conduit for wisdom, a trait revered in Druidic culture where knowledge and insight were prized above all.

In conclusion, the Rowan tree's exalted status in Druidic tradition stems from its potent symbolism, protective attributes, and pivotal role in rituals and mythological narratives. As the Witchwood, the Rowan exemplifies the Druidic approach to the natural world—a world infused with meaning, alive with spirits, and vibrantly interconnected. The reverence afforded to the Rowan tree reflects a broader Druidic worldview, one that recognizes and venerates the mystical dimensions of the plant kingdom.

CHAPTER 8: PLANTS IN DRUIDIC DIVINATION

The ancient Druids, revered for their profound connection with nature, held a deep-rooted belief in the mystical attributes of plants. Their practices were imbued with an intrinsic understanding of the natural world, which they harnessed in their divinatory rituals. This chapter delves into the enigmatic realm of Druidic divination, unearthing the significant roles that plants played in these esoteric practices. From leaves to roots, the Druids perceived every part of a plant as a potential conduit to the divine, offering insights into the future and the hidden truths of the present.

The Symbiosis of Flora and Future

In the world of Druidic divination, plants were not merely passive tools but active participants in the revelatory process. The Druids believed that each plant possessed a spirit, an essence that could interact with the forces of the universe. This belief system recognized the interconnectedness of all life forms and the ability of plants to bridge the gap between the physical realm and the metaphysical.

For instance, the practice of reading the patterns of leaves in a bowl of water, known as hydromancy, was not simply an act of random interpretation. It was a nuanced dialogue between the diviner and the plant spirit, with each swirl and arrangement offering a cryptic message to be deciphered. Similarly, dendromancy involved interpreting the rustling of leaves, the sway of branches, and the patterns of bark on trees. Each whisper of the wind through the leaves was perceived as a voice from beyond, a cosmic whisper that could foretell events or provide guidance.

Omens and Auguries: The Language of Nature

The Druids' deep attunement with their environment enabled them to read signs and omens in the natural world. For them, nothing was coincidental; everything held significance. The sudden appearance of a particular plant, the way a leaf fell to the ground, or the unexpected blooming of a flower out of season – all these were seen as messages from the gods, the ancestors, or the spirit realm.

These omens were not taken lightly. They required interpretation, a skill that Druids honed through years of study and practice. The language of nature was complex, and understanding it required not only knowledge of plants and their properties but also an intuitive, almost empathetic connection with the natural world.

Plants as Oracles: The Whispering Herbs

Certain plants held particular significance in Druidic divination. The revered oak tree, for instance, was often seen as a portal to other worlds, its acorns used in various forms of divination. The ash tree, with its sprawling roots and towering height, represented the connection between the upper and lower worlds, and its leaves were used in rituals seeking wisdom and guidance.

Herbs, too, played a crucial role in Druidic divination. Mugwort, known for its dream-inducing properties, was often used in rituals to induce visions and prophetic dreams. Similarly, vervain was considered a sacred herb, its purifying qualities making it ideal for cleansing ritual spaces and tools before divination practices.

The Druids also employed more complex methods, such as geomancy, which involved casting small pebbles or seeds upon the ground and interpreting the patterns they formed. Each plant seed held a specific meaning, and their arrangement provided a cryptic map of future events or answers to pressing questions.

Divination as a Dialogue with the Divine

Druidic divination was not simply a method of fortune-telling; it was a profound spiritual practice. It required a state of heightened awareness, a deep reverence for the natural world, and an openness to the mysteries of the universe. Through their intimate relationship with plants, Druids sought not only to glimpse the future but also to understand the underlying currents that shape our existence.

In essence, plants were seen as allies, guides, and oracles, offering a connection to a world beyond the physical. They were the medium through which the Druids engaged in a dialogue with the divine, seeking wisdom, guidance, and a deeper understanding of the cosmos.

Summary

This exploration of plants in Druidic divination reveals the intricate and intimate relationship the ancient Druids had with the natural world. Viewing plants as living entities with spirits and voices, they engaged in practices that transcended mere prediction, seeking instead a harmonious dialogue with the forces of nature. Their divinatory rituals were profound spiritual engagements, ones that continue to fascinate and inspire those drawn to the ancient mysteries of Druidism.

CHAPTER 9: HERBS FOR HEALING: A DRUIDIC PHARMACY

The Druidic tradition, steeped in mystery and reverence for the natural world, held a profound understanding of the healing virtues of plants. This chapter delves into the verdant apothecary of the Druids, a cornucopia of botanicals employed not only for their physical curative properties but also for their spiritual and emotional resonance. Through a lattice of lore and practical wisdom, we uncover the Druidic approach to healing, one that intertwines the corporeal with the celestial, manifesting an ancient form of holistic medicine.

Druidic Healing Philosophy

Druids perceived wellness as a harmonious balance between the physical, mental, and spiritual aspects of a person. Their healing practices were deeply rooted in an intuitive understanding of the natural world, emphasizing a symbiotic relationship between humans and plants. This principle extended beyond mere symptom treatment; it sought to realign the individual with the natural order, thereby restoring equilibrium. Their holistic approach was not merely an intervention but a preventative modality, entwining diet, lifestyle, and spiritual practices.

The Druidic Materia Medica

The Druidic herbal compendium was extensive, each plant carefully selected for its therapeutic and energetic attributes. Some of the quintessential herbs included:

- **Vervain (Verbena officinalis)**: Revered as a sacred herb, vervain was a cornerstone of Druidic medicine. It was considered a panacea, believed to fortify the nervous system, alleviate digestive disorders, and act as a tranquilizer. Its spiritual significance was paramount, often used in purifying rites and to forge a connection with the divine.

- **Yarrow (Achillea millefolium)**: This versatile herb was a staple in the Druidic pharmacy. Yarrow's astringent properties made it invaluable for wound healing, and it was also used to reduce fevers and treat various internal ailments. Symbolically, yarrow was associated with divination and was often utilized in rituals seeking insight.

- **Meadowsweet (Filipendula ulmaria)**: Meadowsweet, with its pleasant aroma and gentle properties, was used to treat a variety of ailments, including colds, acid reflux, and inflammation. It was a testimony to the Druids' advanced understanding of herbal properties, as meadowsweet contains salicylic acid, the precursor to aspirin.

- **Bilberry (Vaccinium myrtillus)**: These dark berries were highly esteemed not only for their nutritive value but also for their medicinal properties. Bilberries were consumed to enhance vision, especially night vision, and to treat gastrointestinal issues.

- **Nettle (Urtica dioica)**: Often considered a weed in modern times, nettle was a plant of significant worth to the Druids. It was used to detoxify the body, treat arthritis, and as a tonic for its rich mineral content.

The Integration of Ritual in Healing

Druidic medicine was not confined to the physical administration of herbs. It was a process infused with ritual, a way to invoke the plant's spirit and harmonize it with the patient's energy. The Druids believed that each plant possessed a spirit or essence that contributed to its healing powers. The collection of herbs was conducted with great reverence, often involving rituals that included offerings and chants to honor the spirit of the plant.

The preparation of remedies was equally ritualistic, sometimes aligning with specific lunar or solar phases to enhance the plant's potency. These concoctions were not mere extractions but alchemical blends imbued with intention and prayer, a fusion of earthly and ethereal wisdom.

In conclusion, the Druidic pharmacy offers us a window into an ancient system of healing that transcends the mere biochemical properties of plants. It invites us to consider a more holistic, interconnected approach to health, one that honors the symbiotic relationship between humans and the natural world. As we delve deeper into the verdant realm of Druidic herbalism, we uncover layers of wisdom that resonate with modern holistic practices, reminding us of the timeless dance between nature and well-being.

CHAPTER 10: PLANTS IN DRUIDIC RITUALS AND FESTIVALS

Within the verdant embrace of Druidic practices, plants not merely exist as passive flora but emerge as potent agents, woven into the very fabric of rituals and festivals. This chapter delves into the entwined relationship between plants and the Druidic calendar, unveiling the roles these vegetal entities play in the cyclical celebrations and rites that mark the passage of seasons and significant life events.

The Seasonal Tapestry and Plant Rites

The Druidic year, segmented into a tapestry of festivals, reverberates with the cycles of nature. Each festival, be it Samhain, marking the onset of winter, or Beltane, heralding the fertility of spring, is intricately interlaced with specific plants, elevating their roles beyond mere symbols to active participants in the rituals.

For instance, during Imbolc, the stirrings of spring are welcomed with the blooming of snowdrops, which are woven into garlands and placed upon altars, their pristine whiteness embodying purity and renewal. Conversely, Samhain is a time for reflection and honoring ancestors, where the druids employed the use of herbs like mugwort and yew, plants connected with the veil between worlds, in their ceremonies to enhance spiritual communication and remembrance.

Rites of Passage and Plant Allies

The Druids perceived life as a series of passages, each sanctified through rituals. At the heart of these rites, plants were omnipresent, not only as decorations but as essential components imbued with specific energies and meanings.

In naming ceremonies, for instance, an oak sapling might be planted alongside a newborn, symbolizing strength and endurance. Similarly, during marriage ceremonies, known as handfastings, couples would often exchange rings made of ivy, representing the eternal bond and intertwining of their lives. Furthermore, at the end of life's journey, plants such as yew and rowan, connected to transition and protection, were integral to funerary rites, guiding the departed on their journey to the Otherworld.

The Agrarian Cycle and Druidic Symbiosis

The Druids existed in close symbiosis with the land, and their agricultural calendar was punctuated by festivals celebrating key moments in the farming cycle. Plants were not only the object of these celebrations but were recognized as sentient partners.

During Lughnasadh, the first harvest festival, grains like wheat and barley were not merely reaped but honored for their sacrifice. Corn dollies, intricate figures woven from the last sheaf of the harvest, were created as embodiments of the grain spirit, ensuring its return the following year. This deep recognition of the life force within plants encapsulates the Druidic belief in the cyclicity of life, death, and rebirth.

Summary

In the Druidic world, plants were far more than passive fixtures in rituals and festivals; they were active, vibrant participants. Through seasonal celebrations and rites of passage, the Druids acknowledged the profound connections between the human and plant realms, weaving a tapestry of mutual respect and symbiosis. This intricate relationship underscores the reverence Druids held for the natural world, recognizing the cycles of life and the pivotal role plants play in them. As we explore this verdant landscape, we glean not only historical insights but also timeless lessons on harmony and balance with the natural world.

CHAPTER 11: WILLOW: THE TREE OF DREAMS

In the verdant tapestry of Druidic herbalism, each plant and tree occupies a sacred niche, imbued with its own mystical properties and spiritual significance. Among these, the willow tree whispers its secrets on the wind, its lithe branches dancing in the moonlight, a conduit for dreams and the esoteric wisdom of the ancients. In this chapter, we delve into the enchanting realm of the willow, exploring its role in dream divination, its place in the Druidic herbal lexicon, and the enigmatic practices that surround this ethereal tree.

Willow: The Ethereal Custodian of Dreams

The willow, with its graceful, cascading branches and leaves, has long held a special place in the hearts of the Druids. Known as 'Saille' in the Ogham script, the willow is deeply connected to water, embodying the fluidity of intuition and the subconscious mind. Its proximity to water bodies and its penchant for thriving in damp environments only deepen its associations with the dream world—a realm that, like water, is mutable, profound, and essential for life.

Druids believed that the willow possessed the ability to bridge the waking world with that of dreams and visions. Its role as a facilitator of dream divination is particularly notable. Practitioners would seek the solace of willow groves, resting in their sanctified shade, to receive prophetic dreams or commune with the spiritual realm. These nocturnal rituals, shrouded in the gossamer veil of mysticism, were instrumental in decision-making, gaining insight, and connecting with the divine.

Enigmatic Practices: Willow in Rituals and Lore

The willow's flexible branches and propensity for regeneration —where even a fallen branch could take root and flourish anew—made it a symbol of adaptability and resilience. These characteristics were mirrored in the rituals that entwined willow into their fabric. During ceremonies of healing or spiritual growth, the Druids would craft wreaths and garlands from willow branches, invoking its restorative energy.

In addition to its use in rituals, the willow held a prominent place in Druidic lore. It was said that spirits and deities favored the willow, often residing within or near these sacred trees. Offerings and prayers would be made at the base of ancient willows, their gnarled trunks and sprawling roots perceived as gateways to other realms or as anchors for celestial energies.

Dream Divination: Techniques and Symbolism

The practice of dream divination, or oneiromancy, under the willow was an intricate process that began with meticulous preparations. Participants would fast and meditate, purifying their bodies and minds to heighten their receptivity to the ethereal messages conveyed in dreams. As night descended, they would lie beneath the willow, allowing its gentle sway to lull them into slumber.

In the dreamscape, willows often appeared as symbols of transformation, guardianship, and healing. Interpreting these visions was an art in itself, requiring profound understanding of both the natural world and the subconscious mind. Dreams of willow might portend a period of change or growth, a need for emotional healing, or the presence of a protective force in one's life.

The act of interpreting these dreams was not taken lightly. It was understood that the insights gleaned from the embrace of the willow were gifts from the spiritual realm, to be treated with reverence and contemplation. The Druids believed that dreams held the keys to understanding the self, the universe, and the intricate web of life that connected all beings.

In conclusion, the willow, with its dream-like qualities and deep-seated connections to the esoteric, serves as a testament to the Druids' profound relationship with the natural world. Its role in dream divination and mystical practices is a poignant reminder of the enigmatic and intertwined paths of nature, spirituality, and the human psyche. As we close this chapter on the willow, the Tree of Dreams, we carry forward its lessons of resilience, transformation, and the boundless depths of our own dreams and visions.

CHAPTER 12:
HERBAL AMULETS
AND TALISMANS

In the tapestry of Druidic tradition, the warp and weft of mystical plant lore weave a compelling narrative. Among the myriad practices, the crafting of herbal amulets and talismans stands as a testament to the Druids' deep understanding of the esoteric properties of plants. This chapter delves into the profound relationship between Druidic practices and the use of plant-based amulets for protection, luck, and spiritual connection.

Herbal Amulets: Protective Companions

Amulets, by their very essence, are objects charged with protective properties, often worn on the body or placed in sacred spaces. In the Druidic lexicon, these are not mere ornaments but potent symbols, imbued with the energy of the plants from which they are crafted. The Druids harnessed specific plants for their inherent virtues; for instance, a sprig of rowan, known as the Witchwood, was commonly used to ward off malevolent forces due to its strong protective aura. Similarly, the wood of the oak, revered for its robustness and longevity, was fashioned into charms to endow the bearer with strength and resilience.

The process of creating these amulets was imbued with

ritualistic fervor. The Druids believed that the act of harvesting the plant material was as crucial as the crafting itself. It was done with reverence, often at auspicious times such as the full moon or during specific sabbats, to ensure that the amulet was infused with the most potent energies.

Talismans: Embodiments of Intent

While amulets served as protective wards, talismans were created with a different purpose: to attract certain energies or manifest specific intentions. These objects, often inscribed with symbols or Ogham script, were considered dynamic and active, as opposed to the passive nature of amulets. For instance, a talisman made from mistletoe, especially when cut with a golden sickle during the Winter Solstice, was believed to attract love and fertility.

The Druids' profound understanding of plant properties allowed them to tailor talismans to an individual's needs. They considered not only the physical aspects but also the symbolic, metaphysical properties of plants. By combining different materials, they could concoct a powerful item designed to bring forth a particular outcome or support a personal journey.

Plant Spirits and Energetic Imprints

Central to the creation of these mystical items was the belief in the spirit or essence of the plant. Druidic practitioners engaged in deep communion with these spirits, often through meditative practices or offerings, to seek their blessings in the crafting process. It was a symbiotic relationship; the plant spirits were honored and, in return, lent their energies to the amulets and talismans.

Moreover, the Druids were adept at imbuing these objects with their own intentions through rituals and incantations.

The energetic imprint of their thoughts, desires, and will was meticulously transferred, aligning the object's vibration with the intended purpose. This process transformed a simple plant item into a powerful ally, carrying the force of both the plant spirit and the practitioner's focused intent.

The Continuation of Tradition

Even today, the echoes of these ancient practices reverberate in modern Druidic and neo-pagan circles. The creation of herbal amulets and talismans continues, albeit adapted to contemporary contexts. The core principles, however, remain unchanged: reverence for plant spirits, understanding of their properties, and the meticulous crafting process.

The creation of an herbal amulet or talisman is far more than a physical act; it is a dance of energies, a communion with the natural world, and a manifestation of will. It symbolizes the enduring connection between the Druids and the mystical plant kingdom, a relationship that is both protective and empowering.

This chapter has shed light on the intricate world of Druidic herbal amulets and talismans, unraveling the layers of symbolism, ritual, and belief that make these objects far more than mere trinkets. They are the tangible embodiments of a profound spiritual wisdom that understands the deep interconnectedness of all life, with plants serving as powerful allies in the journey of protection, transformation, and manifestation

CHAPTER 13: YEW: THE TREE OF TRANSFORMATION

In the annals of Druidic lore, the Yew tree occupies a revered and awe-inspiring place. Known scientifically as Taxus baccata, this coniferous arboreal being has been emblematic of mystique and metaphysical metamorphosis across the variegated tapestry of Druidic traditions. This chapter delves into the manifold dimensions of the Yew, unraveling its symbolic connotations, its roles in rituals, and its profound connection with the concepts of death and rebirth.

The Symbolic Yew: Death and Eternity

The Druids, steeped in an understanding of the cyclical nature of life, discerned in the Yew a profound emblem of continuity and transformation. Unlike many other trees, the Yew does not surrender to the seeming finality of death; rather, it transcends it. Even when its central trunk decays, it can regenerate itself, sending up new shoots, hence symbolizing resurrection and eternal life. This ability made it a sentinel of graveyards, often planted to watch over the repose of souls, embodying a bridge between the terrestrial and the ethereal realms.

The Yew in Rituals: Gateway to the Otherworld

In the Druidic rituals, the Yew's presence was deemed quintessential. It was often associated with Samhain, a festival marking the end of the harvest season and the commencement of the darker half of the year. This period was believed to be a liminal time when the veil between worlds was thinnest. Branches of Yew were used to decorate altars, its wood to craft magical staves and wands, acting as talismans that facilitated communication with ancestral spirits and deities of the Otherworld.

Moreover, the consumption of the Yew's leaves, albeit in highly controlled ceremonial contexts, was said to induce trance states. These trance states allowed the Druids to embark on inner journeys, navigating the intangible landscapes of death and rebirth. Here, the tree acted not merely as a symbol but as a veritable portal, through which profound spiritual transformations were wrought.

The Yew and Immortality: A Druidic Elixir

Beyond its roles in rituals and symbolism, the Yew was believed to harbor secrets to longevity. Ancient Druidic texts, now lost to the mists of time, purportedly detailed recipes of elixirs crafted from the Yew, promising extended lifespans and enhanced spiritual insight. While modern interpretations urge caution —given the toxicity of the tree's berries and leaves—these narratives further cement the Yew's position as a tree not merely of death, but of life persisting beyond the customary bounds.

Conservation and Continuity

Today, the Yew continues to captivate those who walk the Druidic path, and its conservation has become a matter of spiritual import. Ancient Yews, some predating the Common

Era, still stand as silent sentinels in sacred sites across Britain and Europe. Preserving these living relics is seen not merely as an ecological endeavor but as a continuation of the sacred trust between the Druids and their cherished arboreal companions.

In Closing

The Yew, with its deep roots burrowing into the annals of time, remains an enigmatic and potent symbol within Druidic traditions. It is a tree that whispers of endings and beginnings, of cycles that close only to commence anew. In its shadow, one contemplates the profound mysteries of existence, the undying nature of the spirit, and the perpetual dance of transformation that underpins all life. Thus, the Yew stands, not merely as a tree but as a testament to the inexorable continuity that the Druids revered—a continuity that we, too, are a part of.

In the Druidic herbal lexicon, the Yew stands as a paragon, a tree that encapsulates the profound wisdom of an ancient tradition, inviting us to reflect, to learn, and ultimately, to transform.

CHAPTER 14: THE ALCHEMY OF PLANT-BASED POTIONS

Nestled within the Druidic traditions is a profound alchemy, one that transmutes the essence of Earth's flora into potent brews and elixirs. These concoctions were not solely for physical ailments but often served a deeper purpose, acting as keys to unlock spiritual insights and facilitate communion with the natural world. This chapter delves into the beginner's guide to Druidic brews and elixirs, tracing the ethereal threads that bind the physical properties of plants to their mystical applications.

The Essence of Druidic Brews

The Druids, revered as wise and sagacious beings, harnessed the intrinsic powers of plants to create brews and elixirs. These were not concocted haphazardly but followed intricate recipes passed down through generations. The plants chosen for these potions were not random; each had its place in the Druidic herbal lexicon, revered for its unique properties. From the verdant leaves of the mistletoe to the robust bark of the oak, every ingredient was carefully selected, each lending its vibrational essence to the potion.

Brews for Mind, Body, and Spirit

The Druidic potions served a triune purpose: healing the body, elevating the mind, and nourishing the spirit. For physical healing, plants known for their medicinal properties were often used. Herbs like yarrow, known for its ability to staunch bleeding, or the willow, whose bark offered pain relief, were common. Yet, these potions were more than mere medicine; they were a conduit to the divine. Elixirs crafted with vervain or meadowsweet were not just for physical ailments but were believed to elevate the consciousness, opening channels to higher wisdom and facilitating profound spiritual experiences.

Rituals and Rites of Passage

Beyond individual use, these plant-based potions played a crucial role in Druidic rituals and rites of passage. They marked significant transitions, from the celebration of seasonal festivals to the solemnity of funerals. A particular brew might be created to honor the transition from winter to spring, imbued with the essence of new growth and vitality. Another might be used in a rite of passage, symbolizing the death of one's former self and the rebirth into a new phase of life. These potions were interwoven with the cyclical nature of existence, echoing the Druidic belief in the interconnectedness of all things.

The Alchemical Process

The creation of these potions was a sacred act, steeped in ritual and reverence. It began with the ethical harvesting of plants, done with respect for the Earth and acknowledgment of the plant's sacrifice. The Druids believed in asking permission from the plant spirits and offering gratitude for their gifts. The preparation of the brews was equally hallowed, often performed under specific celestial alignments or within consecrated spaces, imbuing the potions with celestial energies and amplifying their potency.

Modern Reverberations

Though the ancient Druids walked the Earth long ago, the echoes of their plant-based alchemies still reverberate in modern practices. Contemporary herbalists, though perhaps not adhering strictly to Druidic traditions, honor the spirit of these ancient practices through their deep respect for plant wisdom and the healing powers of nature. As we explore these ancient potions, we glean insights into the profound connection our ancestors perceived between the Earth and the cosmos—a connection that remains as potent today as it was in the days of the Druids.

In this chapter, we have embarked on a foundational exploration of the Druidic brews and elixirs, touching upon their physical, mental, and spiritual applications. We have glimpsed into the rituals surrounding their creation and the profound respect the Druids held for the plants that provided their essence. As we continue our journey through the mystical plants of Druidic traditions, we carry with us an understanding of the intricate alchemy that transforms the humble offerings of the Earth into vessels of profound wisdom and connection.

CHAPTER 15: FERNS AND MOSSES: THE LESSER-KNOWN MYSTICS

In the shadowy understory of the ancient groves, where light filters through a canopy of leaves and branches, a different kind of magic thrives. Here, beyond the reach of the sun's full glare, ferns unfurl their fronds, and mosses carpet the earth in velvety green. In Druidic traditions, while towering oaks and mystical mistletoe have claimed much of the lore and limelight, ferns and mosses hold their own unique and often overlooked significance.

Ferns: The Green Chronomancers

Ferns, with their prehistoric lineage stretching back over 360 million years, are the venerable elders of the plant kingdom. In Druidic traditions, ferns are often associated with time, secrecy, and the unfolding mysteries of existence. Their uncurling fronds, reminiscent of a slowly revealing scroll, have been likened to the gradual unfolding of wisdom and knowledge over time. In many cultures, ferns are also symbols of luck, protection, and eternal youth, traits that resonate with their ability to survive and thrive in shadowy forests and glades.

In Druidic practices, certain species of ferns were used for their purported magical properties. For example, the bracken fern was believed to have the power to render one invisible when worn or carried, reflecting the fern's own elusive nature, often hidden beneath the forest's canopy. The myth of the "fern seed," which could only be collected during the Midsummer's Eve and possessed potent magical qualities, is another testimony to the mystique surrounding these plants.

Mosses: The Silent Storytellers

Mosses, often found sharing the same damp and shaded habitats as ferns, are the humble custodians of the forest floor. These ancient plants, which lack the conventional flowers and seeds of their botanical brethren, have a subtle yet profound presence in Druidic symbolism. Moss, with its quiet, unassuming growth and its capacity to thrive in places where other plants might falter, symbolizes resilience, healing, and the nurturing of growth in adverse conditions.

The velvety carpets of moss that drape over stones and tree trunks are also seen as storytellers, whispering tales of the forest's history. In their silent, steady growth, they hold memories of the woods, recording the passage of time and the cycles of life and death in their simple, green tapestries.

In practical terms, mosses were valued for their medicinal properties and as a source of comfort. Sphagnum moss, for example, has notable antiseptic properties and was used as a wound dressing. Its capacity to hold large quantities of water made it an invaluable resource for both healing and survival in the wild.

The Role of Ferns and Mosses in Rituals

In Druidic rituals, ferns and mosses played more subtle, yet integral roles. Ferns, with their connotations of time and unfolding wisdom, were sometimes incorporated into rites of passage and ceremonies that marked significant life transitions, serving as a symbol of the gradual revelation of life's purpose and direction.

Mosses, owing to their associations with healing and resilience, were used in rituals that focused on restoration and rejuvenation. Their presence in sacred spaces served as a reminder of the nurturing and regenerative powers of nature, even in the darkest and most inhospitable corners of the forest.

Conclusion

Ferns and mosses, the lesser-known mystics of the forest, hold a special place in Druidic traditions. Their symbolism and uses are as varied and profound as those of the more celebrated plants, offering a unique glimpse into the subtler aspects of Druidic herbal lore. In the verdant stillness of the grove, they remind us that wisdom, magic, and healing can be found in the quietest and most unassuming of places.

CHAPTER 16:
FLOWERS IN DRUIDIC FOLKLORE

The role of flowers in Druidic folklore is as variegated and profound as the petals of a blooming wildflower meadow. Unlike their arboreal cousins, which stand with towering majesty and permanence, flowers have always held a place of delicate impermanence in Druidic culture. This chapter unfurls the petals of meaning and symbolism surrounding flowers in the verdant realms of Druidic myth and practice.

The Language of Flowers

Druids, with their profound connection to the natural world, perceived flowers not merely as decorative elements but as vital communicators in the tapestry of life. Each blossom was a word, a note in a symphony of silent whispers echoing the sacred. In their floral lexicon, the Druids ascribed meanings and messages to flowers, a botanical language through which they could interpret the whispers of the earth and sky.

For instance, the foxglove, with its speckled bell-shaped flowers, was seen as a magnet for faerie folk, its Gaelic name translating to "folk's glove." It was considered a plant of boundary and transition, emblematic of the liminal space between mundane and magical realms. The snowdrop, one of the first flowers to pierce the winter's frost, symbolized hope and the stirring of life's forces under the frozen stillness. Similarly, the primrose, which carpets the woodland floors in spring, was associated with youth and renewal, its pale yellow blossoms like the first gentle rays of dawn.

Floral Participants in Ritual and Rite

Flowers, with their fleeting lifespans and ephemeral beauty, were symbolic participants in many Druidic rituals. Their transient nature reminded Druids of life's fleeting moments, encouraging mindfulness and the cherishing of the transient. During rituals of passage, such as handfasting ceremonies or celebrations of birth, flowers like daisies and violets were woven into garlands and crowns, signifying purity, love, and new beginnings.

The Druidic festival of Beltane, heralding the arrival of summer, saw the countryside ablaze with the vibrant colors of wildflowers. It was a time when the Earth was adorned in her most resplendent attire, and the Druids mirrored this floral tapestry by decorating their homes, altars, and even livestock with garlands of flowers, inviting fertility, protection, and abundance.

Mystical and Medicinal

In the realm of healing, flowers held a distinguished place in the Druidic apothecary. The Druids, astute observers of nature, noted not only the physical healing properties of flowers but also their emotional and spiritual influences. Lavender, with its soothing fragrance, was used to calm the mind and promote peaceful sleep, while the borage flower, with its star-shaped blooms, was considered a balm for the heart, lifting spirits and fostering courage.

The mystical properties of flowers were equally esteemed. The elderflower, for instance, was thought to be guarded by the Elder Mother, a tree spirit who presided over the threshold between worlds. A tea made from its flowers was believed to enhance visionary experiences and open the gates to otherworldly realms.

Summary

In Druidic tradition, flowers are far more than botanical specimens; they are the delicate threads weaving together the realms of the physical and spiritual, the earthly and the ethereal. They are symbols, healers, and guides in the great tapestry of existence. As our exploration of flowers in Druidic folklore concludes, we are reminded of the wisdom that lies in observing and understanding the subtle language of nature, a language in which every petal and leaf has a story to share.

CHAPTER 17: SYMBOLISM AND METAPHYSICS OF DRUIDIC PLANTS

In the verdant realm of Druidic traditions, plants are not merely silent witnesses to the passage of time or simple repositories of medicinal compounds. Rather, they are imbued with a profound symbolism and metaphysical significance that offer a deeper insight into the Druidic worldview. As we venture into this intermediate exploration, we delve into the rich tapestry of meanings and the metaphysical aspects that these mystical plants embody in Druidic traditions.

The Language of Symbolism in Plants

The Druids perceived the natural world as a living, breathing entity, with each plant holding a unique message and symbolism. Trees, for instance, were not just organisms producing oxygen; they were sacred beings. The oak, with its enduring strength and towering presence, symbolized endurance, stability, and protection. Its wide-reaching branches were seen as arms stretching towards the heavens, creating a connection between the earthly realm and the divine.

Mistletoe, with its curious habit of growing without soil, was seen as a bridge between worlds – an intermediary between the celestial and terrestrial. Its ability to blossom even in the harshest of winters made it a symbol of resilience and eternal life. Rowan, with its fiery red berries, was considered a ward against malevolent forces, representing protection and insight.

This language of symbolism extended beyond trees to all forms of plant life. Even the humblest of mosses whispered ancient secrets of persistence and adaptability, growing in places where other plants could not. Flowers, with their myriad colors and forms, were messages from the divine, each bloom holding a distinct meaning in the complex lexicon of Druidic flora.

Metaphysical Dimensions of Druidic Plants

Beyond their symbolic representations, plants in Druidic traditions were also viewed through a metaphysical lens. They were believed to possess an intrinsic essence or spirit that transcended their physical form. This belief stemmed from the Druidic understanding of the interconnectedness of all life, where every creature, rock, and plant was considered a vital thread in the tapestry of existence.

In Druidic rituals, plants were used not only for their physical attributes but for their metaphysical qualities as well. The act of incorporating a particular plant into a ritual was a way of invoking its spirit, drawing upon its unique energies to enhance the potency of the rite. It was a dance of synergy, where the metaphysical properties of the plants interwove with the intentions of the practitioner to create a harmonious manifestation of will.

The concept of 'anima loci', the spirit of the place, was central to Druidic belief. Sacred groves were more than collections of trees; they were living sanctuaries where the spirits of the land converged. Each grove had its unique vibrational signature, shaped by the plants that resided within it. The Druids were adept at reading these subtle energies, choosing groves with the right resonance for their ceremonies.

The Druidic Herbal Lexicon: An Intermediary Language

As we immerse ourselves in the Druidic herbal lexicon, it becomes apparent that understanding the symbolic and metaphysical attributes of plants is akin to learning a new language. This language, rich in imagery and nuance, allows us to perceive the world through the eyes of the Druids, where every leaf and root tells a story.

The challenge for the intermediate learner is to move beyond the mere identification of plants and their uses, delving into the more subtle aspects of their nature. It involves tuning in to the whispers of the plant spirits, discerning their messages, and comprehending their roles within the greater symphony of nature. It is a journey of deepening connection, where each plant becomes a key to unlocking the mysteries of the Druidic universe.

In this chapter, we have explored the fascinating realm of symbolism and metaphysics in Druidic plants. From the mighty oak to the unassuming moss, each plant holds a wealth of meaning and metaphysical significance that enriches the tapestry of Druidic traditions. As we continue our journey, let us carry with us a newfound appreciation for the language of plants, a language that speaks not in words but in symbols, energies, and spirits – a language that bridges the gap between the mundane and the divine.

CHAPTER 18: ETHNOBOTANICAL INSIGHTS INTO DRUIDIC HERBS

The verdant tapestry of Druidic herbalism is interwoven with ethnobotanical wisdom, encompassing the botanic characteristics, ecological niches, and the symbiotic relationship between plants and humans throughout history. As we delve into the botany behind the mystical flora cherished by the Druids, it's paramount to approach with a sense of reverence for the intricate interplay between these plants and their surroundings, appreciating their role not only in Druidic rituals but in the ecosystem at large.

Botanical Profiles: A Deeper Understanding

Our journey into the ethnobotanical realm begins with a closer examination of the botanical profiles of key plants in Druidic tradition. These profiles encapsulate a comprehensive understanding of plant morphology, lifecycle, and habitat. For instance, the revered oak tree, known in Latin as Quercus, exhibits a robust structure with deep roots and a broad crown. This resilient tree species, which can live for centuries, becomes a symbol of strength and endurance in Druidic culture.

Similarly, mistletoe, or Viscum album, a hemiparasitic plant thriving on the branches of trees, especially apple and oak, represents dependence and interconnectedness, reflecting the Druidic ethos of unity with nature.

Ecological Significance and Human Interactions

Understanding the ecological roles of these plants unveils a tapestry of relationships and dependencies. The oak tree, for example, supports a myriad of wildlife, from the mighty stag to the tiniest insect. It acts as a keystone species, its acorns nourishing a variety of creatures and its canopy providing shelter. Mistletoe, with its evergreen leaves, offers a rare winter sustenance for birds like the mistle thrush, and its white berries are considered a delicacy by many animals, aiding in seed dispersal.

The Druids recognized these ecological dynamics and incorporated them into their practices. They saw the oak tree not just as a symbol of strength but as an integral part of the forest community. Mistletoe, with its ability to thrive on the oak, became emblematic of life's persistence and interdependence.

Ethnobotanical Applications: Beyond Rituals

The Druids' use of plants extended far beyond ceremonial applications. Their intimate knowledge of each plant's properties informed their choices for medicinal and practical purposes. For instance, the bark of the willow tree, rich in salicin, was used to relieve pain and fever, a precursor to modern aspirin. The rowan tree, with its vibrant red berries, served not only as a protective talisman but also as a source of vitamin-rich preserves and infusions.

The interplay of ecological awareness and practical applications reveals a holistic understanding of plants in Druidic society.

Their approach exemplified a sustainable and respectful use of natural resources, predicated on a deep understanding of the flora's ecological roles and life cycles.

Conservation and Modern Implications

In today's context, the Druidic relationship with plants offers profound insights into conservation and sustainability. By understanding the botanical and ecological intricacies of these plants, we can glean lessons on preserving biodiversity and maintaining ecological balance. The oak tree, for example, remains a cornerstone species in temperate forests, and its conservation is pivotal for the health of these ecosystems.

Furthermore, the Druidic practice of observing and interacting with plants with respect and reverence provides a blueprint for modern approaches to conservation. It underscores the necessity of not just understanding the ecological value of plants but also appreciating their cultural and spiritual significance.

As we explore the ethnobotanical landscape of Druidic herbs, we uncover a rich tapestry of botanical knowledge interlaced with ecological insight and cultural wisdom. The Druids' profound connection with the plant kingdom, informed by detailed botanical understanding and deep ecological awareness, serves as a testament to the timeless relevance of their herbal lore. It inspires us to look beyond the surface, to understand the intricate relationships between plants and their environment, and to approach our own interactions with the natural world with the same reverence and respect that characterized Druidic tradition.

CHAPTER 19: THE TREE OGHAM: A SACRED SCRIPT

The Druids, those learned sages of the ancient Celtic societies, were not just keepers of botanical lore; they were also custodians of a unique system of writing known as Ogham. This script, an enigmatic and powerful code, serves as a bridge between the human and arboreal realms. The Tree Ogham, a central aspect of this script, is not just a mere alphabet but a sacred cipher that encapsulates the essences of trees deemed mystical within the Druidic tradition.

The Enigma of the Ogham Script

The Ogham script is composed of a series of marks or notches, traditionally carved into the edges of standing stones or wood staves. This ancient writing system is believed to have been used from the 4th to the 7th century AD, predominantly in Ireland, though examples have been found scattered throughout the British Isles. The script comprises 20 characters, each linked to a specific tree or plant. This correlation is not arbitrary; it is born from the profound symbolic relationships the Druids observed between particular species and various aspects of life, death, and the cosmos.

Each Ogham character is named after a tree or a shrub, and each tree is imbued with rich symbolic meanings and associated with particular myths, divinatory insights, and medicinal properties. This linguistic framework reflects a holistic worldview where language, flora, and the spiritual realm are inextricably interwoven. Understanding the Tree Ogham requires one to step beyond the threshold of the merely literal and into a domain where symbols and metaphors are the primary currencies of communication.

The Mystical Trees of the Ogham

The Ogham script is divided into several aicmí, or groups, each containing characters that hold individual as well as collective significance. Let's delve into some of these revered tree symbols and their corresponding Ogham characters:

1. **Birch (Beith):** Symbolizing new beginnings and purification, birch is the first character of the Ogham and fittingly represents the start of the druidic year. Its association with renewal and cleansing is deeply rooted in Celtic mythology.

2. **Hazel (Coll):** Linked to wisdom and inspiration, hazel is often connected to the pursuit of poetic and prophetic insights. It's said that the hazelnuts of knowledge fell into the well of wisdom, to be eaten by the salmon of knowledge, which were then caught and consumed by the seekers of esoteric wisdom.

3. **Oak (Duir):** The oak is one of the most revered trees in the druidic tradition, symbolizing strength, endurance, and sovereignty. It is associated with the god Dagda, a central figure in Irish mythology, and was often the central tree in the sacred groves where druids held their rituals.

4. **Ivy (Gort):** Representing the search for the self, ivy's ability to bind and connect reflects the

interconnectedness of all life. Its Ogham character invites contemplation of the cyclical nature of existence and the resilience inherent in life's journey.

5. **Reed (Ngetal):** Denoting both directness and flexibility, the reed symbolizes the need for adaptability and clear communication. In a landscape where rigid trees may fall in a storm, the reed bends and survives.

These characters, along with the others in the Ogham script, form a tapestry of wisdom that the druids believed could unlock not only the secrets of nature but also those of the human soul.

Deciphering the Ogham Today

In our contemporary times, the Tree Ogham can serve as a conduit for reconnecting with the ancient wisdom of the druids. Modern seekers and practitioners of druidic traditions often use the Ogham for meditation, divination, and as a mnemonic aid for understanding the properties and lore associated with various trees and plants. Though the full extent of the original druidic practices remains shrouded in mystery, the Ogham script remains a key to unlocking a deeper appreciation for the intricate relationships between language, nature, and the sacred.

The study of the Tree Ogham invites one to a mindful interaction with the environment, fostering a respect for the symbiotic relationship humans share with the natural world. Whether through the creation of personal Ogham staves, the meditation upon the qualities of different trees, or the use of Ogham characters in ritual settings, this ancient script continues to provide a portal through which the wisdom of the druids can flow into modern consciousness.

In this chapter, we've traversed the symbolic grove of the Tree Ogham, exploring its characters, the trees they represent, and their profound symbolic import. The Ogham is more than a mere script; it is a testament to the druids' deep engagement with the natural world and their desire to encapsulate its mysteries within a system of sacred symbols. As we progress further into the intermediate chapters, these threads of symbolism, mythology, and botany will continue to intertwine, revealing the intricate tapestry of Druidic plant lore.

CHAPTER 20: THE INTERSECTION OF DRUIDISM AND SHAMANISM

In the intricate tapestry of ancient spiritual practices, the threads of Druidism and Shamanism weave together, creating a rich and complex picture. This chapter delves into the confluence of these two traditions, particularly in their veneration and utilization of plants, exploring how Druidic plant lore intersects with shamanic practices.

Druidism and Shamanism: Parallel Pathways

Druidism, with its roots firmly planted in the Celtic lands, and Shamanism, a term coined to represent indigenous spiritual practices across the globe, share common ground despite their geographical and cultural distances. Both traditions hold a profound respect for nature and see the natural world as imbued with spirits and divine energy. For the Druids, plants were not merely flora but beings with spirits, energies, and wisdom that could be harnessed in various ways. Similarly, shamanic cultures have always held plants in high regard, often using them as allies in healing, divination, and journeying into other realms of consciousness.

The Druids were known for their deep knowledge of the natural world, especially of trees and plants. This knowledge paralleled the shamanic understanding of plant spirits and their uses in healing and spiritual practices. In shamanic traditions, plants are often considered as teachers or guides, offering insights and healing through their unique vibrations and energies. This concept aligns closely with Druidic beliefs about the inherent wisdom and power of plants.

Plant Spirits: The Nexus of Wisdom

One of the primary intersections between Druidism and Shamanism lies in the concept of plant spirits. For Druids, the spirit of a plant could be communicated with, respected, and learned from. This notion closely parallels shamanic practices, where shamans enter altered states of consciousness to interact with the spirits of plants and seek their guidance or assistance. Both traditions acknowledge that each plant possesses its own unique spirit, characteristics, and healing properties.

In the Druidic tradition, mistletoe, oak, and rowan, among others, were considered sacred, with spirits that held great wisdom and power. Similarly, shamanic cultures might work with plants like ayahuasca, tobacco, or peyote, each seen as a spiritual entity with its own personality and teachings. This reverence for plant spirits underscores a fundamental belief in the interconnectedness of all life and the importance of maintaining a harmonious relationship with the natural world.

Shamanic Journeying and Druidic Divination

Shamanic journeying is a practice where the shaman enters a trance state, often induced by drumming, dancing, or plant-based entheogens, to travel to other realms and communicate with spirits for guidance, healing, or divination. While the

Druids may not have used the same methods, their practices of meditation, ritual, and working with plants like mistletoe suggest they too engaged in forms of journeying or altered consciousness to access wisdom and divine insight.

Plants played a crucial role in these practices, serving as gateways to deeper understanding and communion with the spiritual realms. Whether seeking the wisdom of an oak tree or the vision-inducing power of a sacred mushroom, both Druids and shamans understood that plants could open doors to other worlds and facilitate profound spiritual experiences.

Healing Wisdom: The Shared Heritage

Healing is another area where Druidism and Shamanism converge. In both traditions, plants are more than just physical remedies; they are holistic healers that work on the body, mind, and spirit. The Druids were known for their extensive knowledge of herbal remedies and healing practices, a wisdom that was likely shared and influenced by the wider shamanic world.

This shared heritage is evident in the use of similar plants for healing across different cultures. For example, the use of willow bark for pain relief, a practice known in both Druidic and various shamanic traditions, reflects a common understanding of the medicinal properties of plants. This indicates that, despite their cultural differences, both Druids and shamans recognized and harnessed the healing power of plants in comparable ways.

Conclusion

The intersection of Druidism and Shamanism in the realm of plant lore represents a confluence of wisdom and spiritual practices that transcend time and geography. Both traditions, though distinct in their cultural expressions, share a profound reverence for the natural world and understand the intricate relationships between humans, plants, and the divine. By exploring this intersection, we gain a deeper appreciation for the universal threads that connect different spiritual practices and the timeless wisdom that plants have to offer.

CHAPTER 21: UNDERSTANDING PLANT SPIRITS

In the intricate tapestry of Druidic beliefs, the notion of plant spirits—or vegetative deities—occupies a central space. It's a concept that seems to whisper in the rustling leaves and to hum with the rhythm of nature itself. The Druidic tradition holds that each plant is not just a passive, inanimate entity but a vibrant, living presence, each with its own spirit or consciousness. This chapter delves into this intermediate-level discussion on the concept of plant spirits in Druidism, weaving together the threads of mythology, spirituality, and the profound relationship between the Druids and the botanical world.

The Essence of Plant Spirits

To understand plant spirits in Druidism, one must first immerse oneself in the worldview that perceives all elements of nature as interconnected and ensouled. In this perspective, plants are seen as sentient beings with their own will, purpose, and wisdom. The Druidic belief in animism—the notion that all objects, places, and creatures possess a distinct spiritual essence—sets the foundation for the veneration of plant spirits.

These spirits are not merely abstractions; they are the very life force that animates each plant. In the Druidic tradition, the plant spirit is believed to govern the growth, healing properties, and the life cycle of its physical manifestation. It is a custodian of sorts, a consciousness that provides the plant with its unique characteristics and its role within the larger ecosystem.

Communicating with Plant Spirits

The Druids developed intricate practices to communicate with and honor these spirits. Through rituals, meditative practices, and offerings, Druidic practitioners sought to align themselves with the vibrational essence of plants. They believed that by doing so, they could tap into the profound wisdom and healing properties that each plant spirit held.

The process of communicating with plant spirits often involved entering a trance-like state, usually facilitated by rhythmic chanting, drumming, or the use of visionary herbs. In this altered state of consciousness, the Druidic practitioner could commune with the plant spirit, seeking guidance, healing, or knowledge.

The Role of Plant Spirits in Druidic Culture

Plant spirits held a revered place in Druidic culture, and their influence permeated various aspects of daily life. They were integral to the Druidic healing practices, where the spiritual essence of the plant was just as important as its physical constituents. The Druids believed that engaging with the plant spirit could amplify the healing properties of the herb and tailor its effects to the needs of the individual.

In rituals and ceremonies, plant spirits were invoked for their blessings and protection. Sacred groves were seen as the abodes of powerful plant deities, and entering these spaces was an act of engaging with the profound spirit of the place.

The Pantheon of Plant Spirits

The Druidic herbal lexicon is replete with plants that were associated with specific deities or spirits. For instance, the oak tree was often linked with the god Dagda, a figure associated with strength, protection, and wisdom. The mistletoe, revered for its sacredness, was believed to be inhabited by a powerful spirit that could bestow fertility and life.

Each plant spirit was seen as a unique expression of the divine, with its own domain of influence and area of expertise. Understanding the specific nature of each plant spirit was crucial for Druidic practitioners, as it allowed them to engage with these entities in a respectful and meaningful way.

In Conclusion

The realm of plant spirits is a testament to the depth and intricacy of Druidic spiritual ecology. It's a realm where each leaf and root is infused with a deeper significance, where the boundary between the physical and the spiritual is fluid and permeable. For the Druids, understanding and engaging with plant spirits was not a mere aspect of their tradition—it was a way of living harmoniously within the vast, living tapestry of nature. As we move forward in our exploration of Druidic traditions, the concept of plant spirits will continue to serve as a foundational thread, intertwining with various other aspects of this rich spiritual heritage.

CHAPTER 22:
ADVANCED DIVINING
TECHNIQUES

In the profound realms of Druidic traditions, divination practices serve as a conduit between the tangible and the ethereal, a bridge to realms beyond the commonplace. Druidic divination, steeped in enigma and intricacy, employs a panoply of methods, many of which are centered around the subtle energies and spirits of plants. This chapter delves into the intermediate guide to complex Druidic divination methods utilizing plants, unveiling the layers of symbolic and metaphysical significance entwined in these ancient practices.

Plant Omen Reading

The Druids believed that the natural world communicated through omens, and plants were no exception. Plant omen reading, or Botanomancy, is an advanced divination technique that involves interpreting the patterns, movements, and growth of plants. The way leaves rustle in the wind, the direction in which a branch grows, or the sudden blooming of a flower could all be portentous.

In this practice, every nuance of a plant's behavior is meticulously observed. For instance, the Druids might consider it a favorable omen if the oak, a tree they held in high esteem, dropped an acorn on a new moon. Conversely, a wilted mistletoe, despite its revered status, could be interpreted as an inauspicious sign. Such readings required not only a profound understanding of each plant's symbolic meaning but also an attunement to the subtler vibrations of the natural world.

Phyllorhodomancy

Phyllorhodomancy is an intricate method of divination that involves listening to the sounds made by leaves, particularly those of the sacred trees, when rustled either by natural forces or by the hands of a diviner. The Druids believed that different sounds carried different messages and insights. This method required a heightened sense of hearing and a deep meditative focus to discern the whispers of wisdom carried on the leaves' rustling.

Dromenon

In the labyrinthine groves, the Druids would often construct dromenons, intricate spiral or circular patterns laid out with stones and plants. Walking these patterns while holding a question in mind, practitioners believed they could attune themselves to the cosmic rhythm and receive answers from the spirit world. The plants chosen for the construction of the dromenon played a vital role, as each species carried specific energies and symbolic meanings that could influence the outcome of the divination.

Divinatory Elixirs

Not all divinatory practices were external; some required ingesting specially prepared elixirs made from visionary plants. While the exact recipes and plants used remain shrouded in mystery, it is known that these elixirs were concocted with the intent to enhance the diviner's psychic faculties. This allowed for a direct communion with the plant spirits and a profound inner journey to gain insights and prophecies. Such practices were not taken lightly and were reserved for the most seasoned Druids who understood the delicate balance between the physical and spiritual realms.

The Plant Seer's Trance

At the zenith of their divinatory practices, a Druid, often referred to as a seer, would enter a trance state to communicate with the plant spirits. This was achieved through a combination of ritualistic dance, repetitive chants, and sometimes the aid of rhythmic drumming. In this altered state of consciousness, the seer could traverse the liminal spaces between worlds, engaging with plant deities and spirits to glean hidden knowledge and prophetic visions.

This practice underscored the belief that plants were not mere passive entities but were imbued with spirits that possessed wisdom beyond human understanding. The trance allowed for a direct dialogue with these spirits, a sacred communion that was central to Druidic divination and cosmology.

In summary, the Druidic approach to divination with plants was not a mere foretelling of the future. It was an intricate tapestry of practices that sought to harmonize human consciousness with the natural world. These advanced techniques required an intimate knowledge of plant lore, an attunement to the subtleties of nature, and an openness to the mysteries that lie beyond the veil of the physical realm. They remind us that the ancient Druids perceived plants not only as sources of medicine or symbols in their rituals but as living entities, allies, and guides in their spiritual and metaphysical explorations.

CHAPTER 23: COMPLEX DRUIDIC RITUALS AND PLANTS

The realm of Druidic rituals is an intricate tapestry woven from the threads of tradition, symbolism, and a profound connection with the natural world. Central to this are the plants, which are not merely passive participants but active conduits of spiritual energy and intention. This chapter delves into the complexities of Druidic rituals, focusing on the role of specific plants and how their unique attributes contribute to these ancient ceremonies.

The Fabric of Rituals

At the heart of Druidic practices lie rituals, a series of symbolic actions performed for a specific purpose, be it to mark seasonal changes, celebrate significant life events, or invoke divine guidance. These rituals are complex in nature, often involving multiple stages, participants, and, most importantly, a variety of plants, each chosen for its specific energy and symbolism.

One could liken a Druidic ritual to an intricate dance, where every step, gesture, and element holds significance. The plants are akin to the dancers, each moving in harmony with the others, their presence amplifying the ritual's intent and facilitating a connection with the divine. This is not a random assemblage but a carefully choreographed arrangement, where each plant is selected for its role and the energy it brings.

The Druidic Herbal Ensemble

In complex Druidic rituals, certain plants are stalwarts, their presence almost mandatory due to their deep-rooted significance in Druidic lore. The oak, revered for its strength and longevity, often takes center stage, symbolizing endurance and stability. Mistletoe, with its mysterious growth and associations with healing and protection, is used to sanctify the space and participants.

However, beyond these well-known plants lies a cornucopia of other botanicals, each adding its unique vibration to the ritual. The rowan tree, with its bright red berries, is a sentinel against negative energies, its presence creating a protective barrier around the sacred space. The willow, supple and resilient, is woven into rituals involving dreams and intuition, its branches often forming the structure of ritualistic tools or altars.

Even less prominent plants, such as ferns and mosses, play their part. These seemingly humble plants are potent symbols of the elusive and the ancient, connecting the participants to the primordial essence of the Earth. In the shadows of these larger plants, they remind participants of the subtlety of nature and the importance of the overlooked.

The Alchemy of Rituals

The complexity of Druidic rituals lies not just in the choice of plants but in their alchemical interplay. When combined, these plants create a synergy, their energies intermingling to form a tapestry of vibrations that resonate with the intended purpose of the ritual.

For instance, in a ritual seeking wisdom and insight, the oak might provide the foundational energy, while the mistletoe elevates the participants' spiritual consciousness. The rowan could act as a guardian, ensuring the purity and sanctity of the wisdom sought. Together, they create a potent amalgamation conducive to divine communication and enlightenment.

Conclusion

Druidic rituals are a testament to the deep connection between the Druids and the plant kingdom. The complexity of these rituals is a reflection of the intricate web of life, with each plant playing a vital role in the spiritual ecosystem. Through understanding the roles and interplay of these plants, one gains not only insight into the rituals themselves but also a deeper appreciation for the profound wisdom embedded in the ancient Druidic traditions.

CHAPTER 24:
SACRED GEOMETRY
IN PLANT LORE

The intricate tapestry of Druidic traditions is woven with threads of mysticism, each pattern enriched by the profound symbolism of plants. Sacred geometry, the metaphysical concept that assigns divine significance to certain geometric shapes and proportions, is a pivotal element in this rich embroidery. In the realm of Druidic beliefs, sacred geometry serves as a transcendent language through which the mysteries of plant lore are not only encoded but also unlocked. This chapter delves into the esoteric relationship between sacred geometry and the Druidic understanding of plant symbolism, revealing the geometric patterns inherent in the natural world and their spiritual resonances within Druidic practices.

The Geometric Essence of Life

Life, in its most fundamental form, is a dance of shapes and patterns. The spiral, one of the most prevalent forms found in nature, echoes throughout Druidic plant lore. From the unfurling of fern fronds to the swirling patterns of sunflower seeds, the spiral is a motif that captures the essence of growth, evolution, and the cyclical nature of existence. The Druids recognized this pattern as a representation of the journey of the soul, mirroring the cosmos's spiraling galaxies and the earth's seasons' circular rhythm.

Another geometric figure deeply revered in Druidic tradition is the circle, embodying the notions of unity, wholeness, and the infinite. Circles are omnipresent in the natural world, from the roundness of fruits to the cycles of the moon that Druids closely observed. In the sacred groves where Druids performed their rites, the circular arrangement of stones or trees formed a sacred space, a microcosm of the universe's harmony.

Geometric Patterns in Sacred Groves

Sacred groves, the sanctuaries of Druidic worship, were not randomly selected plots of land but spaces that resonated with the geometric principles of sacred geometry. The Druids believed that certain groves naturally possessed a geometric harmony that amplified their spiritual potency. The arrangement of trees, the flow of water sources, and the groves' orientation in relation to celestial bodies all conformed to geometric patterns that were thought to be in alignment with the greater cosmic order.

These patterns were not only aesthetically pleasing but also served as conduits for spiritual energies. The Druids utilized the groves' inherent geometry during rituals to enhance their connection with the divine, believing that the alignment of physical space with sacred geometry could bridge the gap between the earthly and the ethereal.

Plant Symmetry and Spiritual Significance

In the Druidic herbal lexicon, the symmetry and structure of plants were considered reflections of the larger cosmic blueprint. Symmetrical patterns in leaves, petals, and branching were not mere coincidences but encoded messages from the divine. The five-pointed star found in the apple's cross-section, for instance, was associated with the five elements—earth, water, air, fire, and spirit—and was considered a symbol of harmony and balance.

Similarly, the intricate geometric patterns of snowdrops and bluebells, often the first to bloom at Imbolc, a Druidic festival marking the beginning of spring, symbolized renewal and the mathematical precision inherent in nature's cycles. The spiral growth of ivy, a plant associated with endurance and the eternal soul, mirrored the journey of spiritual growth, which the Druids believed was a path of ascending spirals, drawing closer to enlightenment with each loop.

Conclusion

The intertwining of sacred geometry and plant lore in Druidic traditions is a testament to the profound interconnectedness the Druids perceived between themselves, their environment, and the cosmos. By deciphering the geometric patterns woven into the very fabric of nature, the Druids sought not only an understanding of the world around them but also a means of aligning their spirits with the divine order. The sacred geometry in plant lore reveals a symbiotic relationship: just as plants follow the geometric principles in their growth and structure, Druidic practices, in turn, harnessed these patterns to achieve spiritual resonance and enlightenment.

CHAPTER 25: CONSECRATION AND DEDICATION OF SACRED GROVES

In the Druidic tradition, the grove holds an eminent place —a sanctum sanctorum where the thin veil between the earthly and the ethereal seems almost imperceptible. These hallowed spaces, often ensconced in the embrace of nature's most venerable trees, are not merely geographical locations but are invested with a profound spiritual significance. The consecration and dedication of these sacred groves is a practice steeped in the rich loam of history and tradition, a rite that imbues these spaces with an aura of the sacrosanct, facilitating a profound communion with the natural world and the divine.

The Sacred Act of Consecration

Consecration in Druidic practice is a multifaceted ritual, a symphony of elements that harmonize to sanctify the grove. This act is not merely a form of blessing but a complex spiritual and metaphysical alignment of the space with the cosmic and natural forces. It begins with a meticulous selection process where the location is chosen based on a plethora of factors, ranging from the types of trees present to the subtle energies and ley lines coursing through the terrain.

Once a site is chosen, a ceremonial cleansing ensues, often through the burning of sacred herbs like sage, juniper, or mugwort, whose smoke is believed to purify and prepare the ground. This is followed by an intricate process of 'marking the boundaries,' a practice wherein the perimeters of the grove are demarcated with symbolic objects or inscriptions, often using the Ogham script. These markings serve as metaphysical barriers, delineating the sacred from the profane and creating a bounded space where the divine might more readily manifest.

Elements of Dedication

The dedication of a sacred grove is an act of profound devotion and is characterized by a series of ritualistic offerings and invocations. The Druids, deeply attuned to the natural world, would ensure that the elements of earth, water, fire, and air are honored and invoked during the ceremony. Water from a nearby spring might be sprinkled around the grove as a blessing and a symbol of life's fluidity and renewal. Fire, contained within a ceremonial brazier, represents the transformative and illuminating power that fuels spiritual insight. Incense, wafting its fragrant tendrils into the air, pays homage to the ethereal realms, and stones or crystals might be laid upon the earth as embodiments of stability and groundedness.

Amidst these elemental tributes, invocations are made to the pantheon of Druidic deities and spirits, beseeching their presence and favor. It is a harmonious entreaty, a chorus of voices that rises from the depths of the grove, echoing through the rustling leaves and intertwining with the whispers of the divine.

The Role of the Community

The consecration and dedication of a sacred grove is not a solitary endeavor but a communal one. It is an event that brings together the community, weaving individual threads into a tapestry of shared spiritual purpose. Each participant plays a role, whether in the crafting of offerings, the chanting of ancient hymns, or the maintenance of the ritual's rhythm through the beat of a drum or the melody of a flute. It is a collaborative act of creation, a moment when the boundaries between self and other blur, and a collective spirit emerges, pulsing with the life force of the grove itself.

In modern times, while the exact details of ancient Druidic consecration rites remain shrouded in mystery, contemporary practitioners draw from the wellspring of historical knowledge and intuitive understanding to recreate these rituals. They are adapted, infused with personal and collective significance, ensuring that the practice remains a living, breathing aspect of Druidic spirituality.

In Summary

The consecration and dedication of sacred groves stand as pivotal rituals within Druidic practice, embodying a deep reverence for the natural world and a yearning for spiritual connection. These rites transform mere plots of land into realms of enchantment, infusing them with a resonance that echoes through the ages. They are acts of remembrance and anticipation, honoring ancient traditions while simultaneously sowing the seeds for spiritual experiences yet to unfold.

CHAPTER 26: SACRED PLANT MUSIC AND POETRY

In the woven tapestry of Druidic tradition, the lyrical and the botanical are threads of a singular fabric, interlaced in a dance of harmony and reverence. This chapter delves into the role of plants within the Druidic musical and poetic spheres, where flora is not merely a subject but an active participant in the cultural expression of the Druids.

The Melodic Whisper of Leaves

In the realm of Druidic music, the voices of plants were not just metaphorical; they were a literal component of the symphony of nature that the Druids sought to harmonize with. The rustling of leaves, the whistling of reeds, and the rhythmic tapping of branches in the wind were considered the Earth's primordial melodies. Druids, deeply attuned to nature, perceived these sounds as integral components of their musical compositions.

Instruments crafted from sacred woods played a pivotal role in translating the voice of the forest into a language understood by humans. Flutes whittled from elder, harps strung with willow, and drums bound with oak skin were believed to carry the essences of their source trees, each instrument resonating with the unique vibrational signature of the plant it was born from. When played in sacred groves, these instruments became conduits for the plants to express their ethereal songs through human hands.

Poetry: Where Words Root and Blossom

Druidic poetry was an intricate interplay of metaphor, allegory, and deep reverence for the natural world. Plants frequently occupied central themes in these lyrical compositions, symbolizing a spectrum of human emotions and universal truths. The oak stood as a steadfast emblem of strength and endurance, while the delicate bloom of the primrose spoke of fleeting beauty and the ephemeral nature of existence.

Moreover, Druidic poets saw themselves as gardeners of words, cultivating verses as one would tend to a garden. Each word was chosen with care, pruned and nurtured until the poem bloomed into its full potential. Poetic recitations were not mere performances; they were acts of devotion, offerings to the plants that inspired them and the divine forces they believed animated all life.

The Alchemy of Song and Seed

The integration of plants into music and poetry served a purpose beyond artistic expression. It was a form of alchemy, an attempt to bridge the mortal and the divine, the human and the natural. Through song and verse, Druids sought to align themselves with the rhythms of the Earth, to enter a state of oneness with the plants that they held sacred.

This alchemical process was believed to imbue the participants with a deeper understanding of the mysteries of life. The act of creating music and poetry was transformative, a ritual that allowed one to touch the sublime and return with a trace of the divine laced in their being. The plants, in turn, were thought to absorb the intentions and emotions of these human expressions, creating a feedback loop of spiritual and creative enrichment.

In conclusion, the Druidic tradition viewed music and poetry as vital forms of communion with the natural world. Plants were not passive subjects but active participants in this cultural expression. Through the sacred interplay of sound and symbol, the Druids sought to weave themselves into the fabric of life, finding unity and understanding within the leafy embrace of the forest.

CHAPTER 27:
VISIONARY PLANTS
IN DRUIDISM

In the mystic tapestry of Druidic practices, one thread that has remained controversial and intriguing is the use of visionary plants. This chapter delves into the historical, ritualistic, and spiritual aspects of these plants within the Druidic tradition.

Historical Context

The Druids, shrouded in the mists of history, left scant direct records of their practices. What is known has been pieced together from archaeological findings, writings of contemporary observers, and the enduring oral traditions of the Celts. Among these fragments of history, there are tantalizing hints that the Druids, like many ancient cultures, may have employed certain plants to alter consciousness and induce visions.

Classical writers such as Pliny the Elder and Strabo mention the use of plants by Druids for prophetic and ritualistic purposes, though their accounts are often outsider perspectives, tinted with the prejudices and misunderstandings of the time. Nevertheless, these accounts, combined with the enduring folklore and herbal knowledge within Celtic lands, suggest that visionary plants held a significant, if enigmatic, role in Druidic practices.

Ritualistic Uses

Visionary plants, according to folklore and hinted at in ancient texts, were possibly used in several Druidic rituals. One such ritual might have been the gathering of mistletoe, a plant held sacred by the Druids. While the primary accounts don't explicitly mention the use of the plant as a hallucinogen, the reverence for mistletoe and its harvesting during specific lunar phases indicate a deeper, possibly psychoactive dimension to its use.

Similarly, the Samhain festival, marking the end of the harvest season and the onset of winter, is believed to have involved practices that altered consciousness. This liminal time, when the veil between worlds was considered thinnest, would have been an opportune moment for the Druids to employ visionary plants in order to facilitate communication with the Otherworld.

Spiritual Significance

In many indigenous and ancient traditions, plants capable of inducing visions are often regarded as sacred. They are seen as bridges between the physical and spiritual realms, allowing shamans, seers, and healers to glean wisdom, seek guidance from spirits, or divine the future. In the context of Druidism, such plants likely served a similar function, providing a conduit to the realms of gods, ancestors, and nature spirits.

This use aligns with the Druidic reverence for nature and their belief in the interconnectedness of all living things. Visionary plants, through their transformative properties, might have been perceived as embodiments of nature's profound mysteries, offering insights not just into the human psyche but also into the intricate web of life that the Druids held sacred.

Controversies and Challenges

The study of visionary plants in Druidism is fraught with challenges. The lack of direct records, the cultural biases of historical sources, and the tendency of modern interpretations to romanticize or misrepresent ancient practices all pose significant obstacles to a clear understanding of the role these plants played. Moreover, the ethical and legal implications of discussing psychoactive substances in a historical and cultural context require careful navigation.

Scholars and practitioners alike must tread a fine line between honoring the historical significance of these plants and avoiding the promotion of their use outside traditional, ritualistic contexts. It's important to emphasize that the knowledge and practices of the ancient Druids were embedded within a specific cultural and spiritual framework that cannot be replicated in the modern world.

Concluding Reflections

The enigmatic nature of visionary plants in Druidism adds a layer of depth to the already rich tapestry of Druidic practices. While the precise details of their use may be lost to the mists of time, the fascination with these plants persists. They serve as a reminder of the ancient Druids' profound connection with nature and their quest for wisdom through the exploration of the inner and outer worlds.

In the next chapters, we will continue our journey through the Druidic herbal lexicon, unraveling the threads of history, myth, and spirituality that weave through this ancient tradition.

CHAPTER 28:
COSMOLOGY AND
THE TREE OF LIFE

The Arbor-Cosmic Nexus

In the tapestry of Druidic tradition, one discerns a profound connection between the macrocosm of the universe and the microcosm of individual life, a connection epitomized in the symbol of the Tree of Life. This arboreal icon is not merely a metaphor but a living embodiment of the cosmos, a sanctified axis mundi that bridges the terrestrial and the celestial. Druidic cosmology, therefore, is not a mere abstraction but a living, breathing paradigm that is rooted deeply within the natural world, and the trees that stand sentinel across the landscapes.

The concept of the Tree of Life transcends mere symbolism. In the Druidic weltanschauung, it is the embodiment of the universe's structure, an organic representation of the cosmos itself. It is both a metaphysical blueprint and a tangible entity, signifying the triadic stratification of the cosmos: the roots delving into the underworld, the trunk representing the middle world of human experience, and the branches reaching upwards towards the celestial realm. This trifold segmentation is a recurring motif in various cultural cosmologies, yet within Druidism, it gains a unique arboreal character, blending the cosmic with the terrestrial.

The Triadic Cosmological Conception

The roots of the Tree of Life extend into the chthonic depths, symbolizing the underworld, Annwn in Druidic lore—a realm of profound mysteries, ancestral spirits, and primordial wisdom. It is not a place of damnation, but rather a subterranean repository of arcane knowledge and the cyclical forces of life, death, and rebirth. Here, the roots absorb the metaphysical nutrients, the ancient wisdom that sustains the entire cosmic organism.

The trunk represents the middle world, the earthly plane of existence, where humans, animals, and plants coexist. It stands as a symbol of stability, connecting the heavens and the underworld, anchoring the cosmic energies in the material realm. The trunk, robust and enduring, is a metaphor for life's journey, marked by the vicissitudes of fate, the ebb and flow of seasons, and the trials and tribulations inherent in mortal existence.

Ascending to the celestial boughs, the branches of the Tree of Life reach towards the empyrean domains, the abode of deities, cosmic forces, and celestial patterns. It is in this ethereal canopy that the Druidic conception of the stars and celestial bodies resides, interwoven with the arboreal branches in a cosmic dendritic pattern. These celestial branches are believed to hold the patterns of fate and the blueprints of destiny, whispered to those who comprehend the silent language of the cosmos.

The Tree as a Cosmic Conduit

The Tree of Life is more than a static symbol; it is an active conduit, a mediator between the different planes of existence. Its leaves, rustled by the cosmic winds, are thought to murmur the secrets of the stars, while its roots resonate with the whispers of the earth. Through rituals, meditations, and contemplations conducted in the presence of these sacred trees, Druids sought to align themselves with the cosmic rhythms, to attune their spirit to the eternal dance of the cosmos.

In this sacred alignment, the individual self is seen as a microcosmic reflection of the Tree, embodying within its soul the same triadic structure that governs the universe. Thus, the journey of spiritual growth is envisioned as an ascent through the Tree, from the roots of personal unconsciousness and primal instincts, up through the trunk of lived experience and social engagement, towards the branches of spiritual enlightenment and cosmic consciousness.

Through the Druidic lens, the arboreal archetype of the Tree of Life is an invitation to explore the mysteries of existence, to perceive the interconnections between all forms of life, and to fathom the intricate tapestry of the cosmos. It is a call to recognize that within every leaf, every branch, and every root lies a cosmic narrative, a fragment of the vast, living cosmos.

In conclusion, Druidic cosmology, as encapsulated in the symbol of the Tree of Life, presents a profound integration of the celestial, the terrestrial, and the chthonic. It is an organic cosmology that breathes with the rhythms of nature, inviting one to explore the depths of the underworld, the complexities of the earthly realm, and the vastness of the celestial sphere. It is a cosmology that is not just understood but experienced through the living symbol of the Tree, a nexus that binds the Druid to the pulsating heart of the cosmos.

CHAPTER 29: DRUIDIC HERBALISM IN MODERN TIMES

As the world advances with leaps and bounds in technology and science, the allure of ancient wisdom, particularly that related to nature and the Earth's healing properties, has not waned. In fact, there is a resurgence of interest in the arcane practices of Druidic herbalism, as people seek a deeper connection with nature and a more holistic approach to health and spirituality. This chapter explores the contemporary manifestations of ancient Druidic herbal traditions and their relevance in modern society.

Relevance in Contemporary Healing Practices

The philosophy and techniques of Druidic herbalism are experiencing a renaissance in the realm of alternative medicine. Modern herbalists and naturopaths often draw inspiration from the holistic approach that Druids took towards healing. This involves understanding the patient's physical, emotional, and spiritual state before recommending herbal remedies. For instance, the use of mistletoe, once revered by the Druids for its healing and protective properties, has found its way into contemporary treatments, albeit with caution and under the guidance of medical professionals, particularly in the realm of oncology.

Furthermore, the concept of "plant spirit medicine," which posits that plants have spirits or energies that can positively affect human health and wellbeing, echoes the Druidic belief in the animistic qualities of plants. This notion is gaining traction among those seeking a deeper, more esoteric connection with the remedies they use, mirroring the ancient Druidic practice of communing with the spirit of a plant before harvesting it for medicinal purposes.

Adaptations in Rituals and Festivals

Druidic festivals, celebrating the seasonal cycles and their associated deities, have found new life in the modern age. Groups like the Order of Bards, Ovates, and Druids organize ceremonies and gatherings that honor these ancient traditions, often incorporating the use of sacred plants like oak, rowan, and willow. These events serve not only as a means of spiritual practice but also as a form of ecological activism, emphasizing the importance of preserving and respecting the natural world.

In these contemporary rituals, there is a conscious effort to adapt ancient practices to modern sensibilities. For example, the ethical sourcing of plants is given priority, reflecting a growing concern for sustainability and environmental stewardship. Additionally, there is an emphasis on personal relevance and psychological healing, demonstrating an evolution from the community-centric rituals of old to a more individualized spiritual experience.

Technological Integration and Druidic Herbalism

In a seemingly paradoxical turn, modern technology has played a significant role in the dissemination and preservation of Druidic herbal knowledge. Online platforms and social media groups allow practitioners and enthusiasts to share information, experiences, and research related to Druidic plants and their uses. This digital network acts as a virtual grove, a community of like-minded individuals dedicated to reviving and preserving ancient wisdom for future generations.

Moreover, the use of technology has enabled a more rigorous study of the properties of plants once held sacred by the Druids. Scientific research can now validate or challenge the efficacy of these plants, leading to a fascinating dialogue between ancient lore and modern science. This synergy not only enriches our understanding of Druidic practices but also contributes to the broader field of herbal medicine.

Druidic Herbalism as a Cultural Touchstone

The enduring fascination with Druidic traditions speaks to a deeper cultural yearning for connection with nature and the past. In a fast-paced, often disconnected modern world, the ancient practices of Druidic herbalism offer a touchstone to a time when humanity lived in closer harmony with the natural environment. By integrating these practices into modern life, individuals find not only a means of physical and spiritual healing but also a sense of continuity with their ancestors and the natural world.

In conclusion, the Druidic herbal traditions, once shrouded in the mists of time, are experiencing a revival in the contemporary era. This resurgence is marked by a respectful adaptation of ancient wisdom to modern sensibilities, a blending of spiritual practice with ecological activism, and a fruitful dialogue between old lore and new science. As we continue to navigate the complexities of modern life, the principles and practices of Druidic herbalism offer a wellspring of inspiration, healing, and connection to the natural world that is as relevant today as it was in the times of the ancient Druids.

CHAPTER 30: DRUIDIC PLANTS IN ALCHEMY

In the heart of ancient alchemical practices, there lies a profound connection with the natural world—a relationship epitomized by the druids and their sacred plant lore. The intertwining of Druidic herbalism and alchemy presents a fascinating tableau, revealing the transformative power of plants not only in physical remedies but also in spiritual metamorphoses. This chapter delves into the arcane relationship between these two esoteric traditions, exploring how Druidic practices influenced and were influenced by the enigmatic art of alchemy.

Alchemical Foundations and Druidic Practices

Alchemy, often misconstrued as the mere pursuit of transmuting base metals into gold, is a profound spiritual discipline. Its roots lie in the quest for the Magnum Opus—the Great Work—an endeavor aiming at spiritual perfection and the attainment of ultimate wisdom. In this pursuit, plants have always held a special place. Druidic herbalism, with its deep understanding of plant properties, energies, and spirits, offered an invaluable repository of knowledge for the alchemist.

The druids, with their intimate knowledge of the natural world, recognized the quintessence or the essential spirit of plants. Alchemists, in their turn, sought to extract and harness these essences to create elixirs, potions, and compounds that could promote healing, longevity, and spiritual awakening. They understood that every plant held a unique combination of the four classical elements—earth, air, fire, and water—and that through alchemical processes, these could be balanced and refined to release the plant's full spiritual potential.

The Role of the Quintessence

A central concept in alchemy is the pursuit of the quintessence, a fifth element or ether, representing the purest form of matter. Druidic herbalists, with their sacred groves and ritualistic approach to plant harvesting, were believed to be adept at capturing this essence. They employed techniques such as timing their harvests with specific lunar phases, conducting rituals to honor the plant spirits, and using particular tools that resonated with the energy of the plants. These methods aligned closely with alchemical practices, which emphasized the importance of celestial influences, ritualistic precision, and spiritual readiness in their operations.

Druidic Contributions to Spagyric Alchemy

Spagyrics, a branch of alchemy focused on plants, owes much to Druidic practices. The term itself, derived from Greek, means to separate and to join together—echoing the alchemical maxim: "Solve et Coagula." This refers to the process of breaking down a substance into its constituent parts (solve) and then recombining them in a purified form (coagula). Druidic herbalists intuitively practiced a form of spagyrics, carefully separating the essential oils, spirits, and physical bodies of plants, and using them in their potions and remedies.

In spagyric alchemy, the essential oil represents the soul of the plant, the alcohol extract symbolizes its spirit, and the remaining ash embodies its body. By recombining these purified elements, alchemists believed they could create a harmonious and potent medicine, infused with the plant's full vitality and healing properties—a philosophy deeply resonant with Druidic beliefs in the holistic nature of healing and the importance of honoring each aspect of the plant.

Alchemical Symbols and Druidic Plant Lore

The rich tapestry of alchemical symbolism often features plants and trees held sacred by the druids. The mighty oak, a symbol of strength and endurance, appears in alchemical texts as a representation of resilience in the face of the transformative alchemical processes. Mistletoe, with its paradoxical qualities of poison and healing, embodies the alchemical principle of duality and the reconciliation of opposites.

Moreover, the Druidic Tree Ogham, a cryptic script associated with trees and plants, shares striking parallels with alchemical symbols. Both systems encode profound spiritual and material knowledge, serving as keys to unlock the deeper mysteries of nature and the cosmos.

Legacy and Modern Interpretations

The symbiotic relationship between Druidic herbalism and alchemy offers rich insights into the ways ancient wisdom traditions approached the natural world. Modern interpretations of this legacy continue to inspire those seeking holistic approaches to healing and spiritual growth. Alchemy and Druidic practices are no longer seen as mere historical curiosities but as living traditions with the potential to deepen our connection with nature and our understanding of the subtle energies that animate the world around us.

This chapter has journeyed through the verdant nexus of

Druidic and alchemical wisdom, exploring how plants serve as a bridge between the physical and the spiritual, the mundane and the mystical. The Druidic influence on alchemy and vice versa reveals a shared reverence for the natural world—a legacy that continues to inspire and inform those on the path of personal transformation and enlightenment.

CHAPTER 31: TOOLS AND INSTRUMENTS MADE FROM SACRED WOODS

In the pantheon of Druidic tradition, trees are not merely passive entities; they are conduits of cosmic wisdom and earthly strength. The Druids harnessed this power, not only through their rituals and medicines but also by crafting sacred tools and instruments from these venerated woods. Each wood, imbued with its unique mystical properties, was carefully chosen to align with the specific purpose of the tool being crafted.

Sacred Wood Selection

The selection of wood for crafting ritualistic tools was an intricate process steeped in the understanding of the inherent qualities of different trees. For example, oak, known for its strength and durability, was often used to create staffs and wands, serving as a direct channel for the Druid's own energy during ceremonies. The oak's association with resilience and wisdom made it a natural choice for instruments that required longevity and spiritual significance.

Similarly, the yew, with its connections to the cycles of death and rebirth, was frequently fashioned into divination rods and mortars for grinding herbs. The belief was that the yew's ability to bridge life and death allowed the user to gain deeper insights during rituals of divination or when preparing medicinal concoctions.

Willow wood, associated with flexibility and the feminine divine, was often carved into harps and flutes. These instruments, used in sacred ceremonies, were believed to channel the willow's ability to connect with emotions, dreams, and the ebb and flow of human experience.

Crafting Ritual

The crafting of these sacred tools was itself a ritual, often conducted under specific celestial alignments or during important dates on the Druidic calendar. The Druids believed that infusing their work with intention and reverence imbued the finished product with greater power. The craftsman would fast, meditate, or perform purifying rituals to ensure that their energy was in alignment with the sacred task at hand.

As the Druid worked, they might chant, pray, or meditate on the intended use of the tool, ensuring that every whittle of the wood or stroke of the brush was a mindful act. It was this combination of the right material, the right timing, and the right intent that charged these objects with their profound mystic energies.

The Life of Sacred Tools

The life of a Druidic tool did not end with its creation. Throughout its use, it would be routinely cleansed, consecrated, and sometimes even 'fed' with oils or other natural substances. This maintenance was both practical, preserving the tool for prolonged use, and spiritual, ensuring that it remained potent and pure for ceremonies.

The tools and instruments made from sacred woods were more than mere objects; they were extensions of the Druids themselves, partners in their spiritual practices, and witnesses to their innermost mystical experiences. They were revered as sacred, and their eventual disposal, often through burial or ritual burning, was conducted with as much solemnity as their creation.

In conclusion, the Druids' creation and use of sacred tools and instruments fashioned from specific woods provides a profound illustration of their deep reverence for nature and their understanding of the mystical qualities inherent in the world around them. These objects were not merely tools but were symbolic of the intertwining relationship between the Druids, their spirituality, and the natural world—a relationship built on respect, harmony, and a profound sense of the sacred.

CHAPTER 32: THE ETHICAL HARVESTING OF DRUIDIC PLANTS

As we delve into the intermediate chapters of our journey through "Mystical Plants in Druidic Traditions," we've come to understand the profound respect Druids held for the natural world. This reverence is not only evident in their rituals and mythologies but also in their practices of harvesting plants. Chapter 32 explores the ethical principles that governed the Druids when they collected plants for their various uses, offering us a template for sustainable interaction with our environment.

Respect for the Living World

The Druidic tradition recognized plants as sentient beings, each with its spirit and agency. This understanding prompted a careful and respectful approach to harvesting. Druids believed that every plant had a purpose and a role within the ecosystem, and removing it without due consideration could disrupt the delicate balance of nature. Therefore, they approached harvesting with a sense of sacred duty, ensuring that their actions did not cause harm to the plant or its surroundings.

Rituals of Permission

Before cutting a branch or plucking a leaf, Druids often performed rituals asking for permission from the plant's spirit. They believed that engaging in a dialogic exchange with the plant's consciousness would lead to a harmonious relationship between the gatherer and the gathered. These rituals could involve offerings, prayers, or moments of silent communication, acknowledging the plant's sacrifice and expressing gratitude for its forthcoming gifts.

Mindful Harvesting Techniques

Druidic harvesting practices were far from haphazard. They adhered to specific techniques designed to ensure the plant's survival and regeneration. For example, when gathering mistletoe, they would never uproot the entire plant, instead of taking only what was needed. Similarly, when harvesting bark or leaves, they employed methods that allowed the plant to heal and continue growing. This meticulous attention to detail ensured that their use of plants was sustainable and that the same plant could continue to provide for future generations.

The Concept of Plant Kinship

Druids often viewed plants not merely as resources to be exploited but as kin, with whom they shared a symbiotic relationship. They understood that their own well-being was intricately tied to the health of the plant world. This sense of kinship discouraged overharvesting and exploitation, fostering a culture of care and stewardship. It was common for Druids to engage in replanting rituals and practices that contributed to the proliferation of plant species, ensuring their availability for years to come.

Contemporary Relevance

In our modern context, where industrial-scale harvesting often leads to environmental degradation, the Druidic approach offers valuable insights. Their practices remind us of the importance of sustainable and ethical interaction with nature. By incorporating principles such as respect, permission, mindful techniques, and kinship, we can develop a more balanced relationship with the plant world, one that honors the earth and contributes to its flourishing.

In sum, Chapter 32 reveals the depth of the Druids' commitment to living in harmony with the natural world. Their ethical harvesting practices serve as a testament to their reverence for plant life and offer us a model for sustainable and respectful interaction with nature. As we move forward into the more advanced chapters, we carry with us the wisdom of these ancient traditions, reminding us of the interconnectedness of all life and the importance of preserving the delicate balance of our planet.

CHAPTER 33: LINGUISTIC TRACES OF PLANT LORE

Language is the fabric through which culture, knowledge, and traditions are woven. In Druidic societies, where oral transmission was paramount, the language held the key to a deeper understanding of the world around them, especially their plant lore. This chapter delves into the linguistic imprints left by the Druids, deciphering ancient texts and languages to unearth the enigmatic world of Druidic plant lore.

Etymological Roots

The etymological exploration begins with tracing the roots of words associated with plants in the Druidic lexicon. Language is an archaeological site, with layers of meaning accumulated over centuries. By delving into the origins of words, one can uncover the lost connections between the Druids and their sacred flora. For instance, the word "druid" itself is believed to stem from the Proto-Celtic *dru-wid-, meaning "oak-knower" or "oak-seer," highlighting the significance of the oak tree in their traditions. This linguistic clue not only reveals the oak's esteemed status but also signifies the Druids' profound knowledge and spiritual connection with their environment.

Deciphering the Ogham

The Ogham script, often referred to as the "Celtic Tree Alphabet," is a cryptic form of writing that flourished among the Druids. Each character, or "few," corresponds to a particular tree or plant, making it a unique botanical cipher. Interpreting these inscriptions is akin to walking through a sacred grove, with each letter a testament to the profound relationship between the Druids and their cherished plants. The Ogham not only encoded botanical knowledge but also served as a medium for preserving spells, incantations, and secrets of the natural world.

Manuscripts and Marginalia

The quest for Druidic plant lore leads us to the margins of ancient manuscripts. In texts like the 'Llyfr Taliesin' (Book of Taliesin) and the 'Lebor Gabála Érenn' (Book of the Taking of Ireland), scholars have unearthed cryptic references to plants used in rituals, healing practices, and divination. The study of these manuscripts is like peering through a keyhole into the past, glimpsing the intricate tapestry of beliefs, rituals, and practices entwined with plant lore.

Linguistic Landscape and Folk Names

The linguistic landscape of the Celtic regions is rich with place names and folk terms that carry echoes of ancient Druidic plant lore. These toponyms and colloquialisms are vestiges of a time when the spiritual and physical landscapes were indistinguishable. By analyzing these names, one can unearth the layers of botanical and mystical significance ascribed to different locales and the flora that inhabit them. For instance, many places in Wales and Ireland have names derived from sacred trees, such as "Derry" from the Irish "Doire," meaning "oak grove."

Reconstructing Lost Knowledge

Language is a portal through which we can access the lost wisdom of the Druids. By piecing together linguistic fragments, we can reconstruct the botanical knowledge that once flourished in Druidic society. This linguistic reconstruction is not merely academic; it is a rekindling of the sacred bond between humans and the natural world—a reminder of the reverence and understanding that the Druids held for their environment.

In conclusion, the linguistic traces of Druidic plant lore are like scattered seeds, holding within them the potential to blossom into a fuller understanding of the Druids' spiritual and botanical wisdom. By studying ancient texts, languages, and etymology, we begin to piece together the mosaic of Druidic plant lore, revealing a world where language, plants, and the sacred were intricately intertwined.

CHAPTER 34: SACRED GEOMETRY AND RESONANCE IN PLANT STRUCTURES

Venturing deeper into the enigmatic realm of Druidic plants, this chapter delves into the intricate dance between sacred geometry, a discipline revering the geometric patterns and harmonic ratios that pervade our universe, and the subtle yet profound resonance found in plant structures. This exploration not only requires a discerning eye but also an openness to embrace the esoteric wisdom that Druidic traditions have safeguarded over the ages.

The Geometric Soul of Plants

At the heart of Druidic belief lies the conviction that all forms of life are infused with a sacred essence, manifesting through patterns that echo the foundational geometries of existence. These geometries, discernible in the spiral of a pine cone, the branching of trees, or the symmetry of a flower's petals, are not mere coincidences but expressions of a deeper cosmic order. This reverence for geometry is not an isolated phenomenon but a thread weaving through numerous spiritual traditions and scientific observations, hinting at a universal code underscoring all of creation.

To understand the relationship between sacred geometry and plants within the Druidic paradigm, one must first acknowledge that geometry is not solely a mathematical discipline but a language through which the natural world communicates its secrets. For instance, the Fibonacci sequence, a series of numbers where each number is the sum of the two preceding ones, manifests conspicuously in the arrangement of seeds in a sunflower or the fronds of a fern. This sequence and the resultant golden spiral are emblematic of growth and harmony, principles that Druidic traditions hold in high esteem.

Resonance: The Symphony of Life

Moving beyond static geometry, resonance introduces the element of vibration into the picture. In the Druidic worldview, each plant is believed to resonate at a particular frequency, contributing its unique note to the symphony of life. This concept parallels modern scientific understanding, where molecular vibrations are recognized as fundamental to the properties of matter. Plants, through their biochemical processes and structural compositions, exhibit distinctive vibratory signatures, which Druids interpret as the plant's spirit or essence.

The notion of resonance in Druidic traditions extends to the belief that humans can attune themselves to the frequencies of different plants, thereby tapping into their inherent qualities and wisdom. This attunement might manifest in various forms, from meditating with a plant to incorporating it into rituals and medicines. The resonance between humans and plants is not merely physical but encompasses emotional, mental, and spiritual dimensions, facilitating a profound communion with nature.

The Interplay of Light and Geometry

An advanced aspect of sacred geometry in plants involves the interaction between light and the geometric structures within plant cells. Chloroplasts, the cellular organelles responsible for photosynthesis, are arranged in patterns that maximize the absorption and utilization of sunlight. The efficiency of this system is not just a triumph of evolution but also a testament to the geometric precision inherent in nature.

Druids, with their keen observation of nature, likely recognized the importance of light in the life of plants and, by extension, the significance of geometric arrangements in optimizing this life-giving interaction. Though they might not have understood the cellular mechanisms as we do today, their veneration for light, geometry, and life echoes our contemporary appreciation for the marvels of photosynthesis.

Conclusion

In embracing the complexities of sacred geometry and resonance in plant structures, this chapter ventures into a domain where science and mysticism converge. The geometric patterns and vibratory qualities of plants are not merely subjects for academic study but portals to a deeper understanding of the interconnectedness of all life. Druidic traditions, with their profound respect for nature, offer a unique lens through which to view these universal patterns, inviting us to consider the possibility that the beauty we observe in the natural world is but a reflection of a grander cosmic order.

CHAPTER 35:
ESOTERIC HERBALISM

In the labyrinthine corridors of Druidic practices, esoteric herbalism represents a rivulet of knowledge that veers into the clandestine recesses of ancient wisdom. This intricate tapestry weaves together elements of ritual, medicine, and metaphysics, revealing the profound depths to which the Druids understood and harnessed the power of plants. As we delve into this chapter, we journey into the heart of Druidic esoteric herbalism, unearthing the secrets that have been shrouded in mystery for centuries.

The Alchemical Fusion

At the core of esoteric herbalism lies the alchemical process of transmuting the mundane into the divine. The Druids believed that every plant possessed a quintessence, a vital spirit that could be extracted, refined, and utilized for spiritual ascension and physical healing. This philosophy of transformation was not solely about changing the physical properties of plants but also about the alchemist's spiritual evolution.

Through intricate rituals, the Druids engaged in what can be termed as "green alchemy." This was the practice of harnessing the elemental energies inherent in plants—earth, air, fire, water, and spirit—to create potions, elixirs, and concoctions that could initiate profound transformations. These were not mere remedies for physical ailments but were believed to facilitate soul-level healing, balance the humors, and aid in achieving a state of equilibrium with the cosmos.

The Secret Language of Plants

Beyond their physical attributes, plants were viewed as repositories of arcane knowledge and wisdom. The Druids developed a secret language, a cipher through which they could communicate with the plant kingdom and decipher the messages held within their verdant forms. This language was not spoken or written in a conventional sense but was a symbiotic exchange of vibrational energies, an intuitive understanding that transcended words.

Through deep meditative practices and rituals, the Druids would attune themselves to the frequency of the plants, entering into a state of oneness with nature. In this communion, plants would reveal their hidden properties, their esoteric uses, and their role within the larger tapestry of the universe. This sacred knowledge was passed down through oral traditions, veiled in myth, and protected by the sanctity of the groves where these esoteric practices were conducted.

The Rituals of Harvesting and Preparation

The process of harvesting and preparing plants for esoteric use was shrouded in ritualistic significance. The Druids adhered to a strict protocol that respected the life force of the plant. Harvesting was often done during specific lunar phases, under certain astrological alignments, and with the utterance of blessings or incantations to honor the spirit of the plant.

Once harvested, the preparation of these esoteric herbs was an art form in itself. The Druids employed a variety of methods— drying, fermenting, distilling, and more—to extract the plants' essence. Each step was imbued with ritualistic intent, and the final product was more than just a concoction; it was a living, vibrational remedy imbued with both the essence of the plant and the spiritual intent of the practitioner.

The Legacy of Esoteric Herbalism

The legacy of Druidic esoteric herbalism extends beyond the annals of history into the realm of the present. Modern herbalists, alchemists, and seekers of ancient wisdom continue to explore these practices, adapting them to contemporary contexts while honoring their sacred origins. The resurgence of interest in plant spirit medicine, vibrational healing, and the metaphysical properties of herbs is a testament to the enduring legacy of the Druids' esoteric herbal knowledge.

In a world where the tangible and intangible intertwine, the practices of esoteric herbalism offer a bridge between the seen and unseen realms. As we walk the path carved by the ancient Druids, we begin to understand that plants are not mere commodities or resources but allies, teachers, and guardians of a wisdom that whispers to us from the verdant heart of nature.

In conclusion, esoteric herbalism represents a profound dimension of Druidic practices, a realm where the boundaries between science, magic, and spirituality blur. It is a testament to the Druids' deep understanding of the interconnectedness of all life and their reverence for the natural world. As we venture forth from this chapter, we carry with us a newfound appreciation for the hidden mysteries that plants hold and the ancient wisdom that continues to illuminate our path.

CHAPTER 36: QUANTUM MYSTICISM IN DRUIDIC PLANT UNDERSTANDING

Bridging the Ancient and the Quantum

In the lush expanse of human understanding, a peculiar entanglement exists between the arcane lore of the Druids and the enigmatic realm of quantum physics. The Druids, with their deep reverence for the natural world, perceived plants not merely as physical entities but as vessels of profound mystical significance. This chapter delves into the fascinating intersection where the ancient wisdom of Druidic plant understanding converges with the contemporary principles of quantum mysticism, a domain where particles dance in uncertainty and consciousness may play a role in the fabric of reality.

Quantum Resonances in Druidic Plant Lore

Quantum physics, in its most fundamental essence, postulates a universe brimming with possibilities, a tapestry woven with probabilities until an observer collapses them into reality. This chimes harmoniously with the Druidic belief that plants are not static beings but dynamic participants in a cosmic play, interacting with the forces of nature and human consciousness. The Druids, in their rituals and meditations, may have unknowingly tapped into the quantum field, engaging with plants at a level beyond mere biochemistry.

The concept of quantum entanglement, where two particles remain connected regardless of the distance separating them, mirrors the Druidic notion of interconnectedness between all forms of life. This principle suggests that the Druids' rituals involving plants could have repercussions extending beyond the observable, touching the very threads of the quantum web that unites the universe. It opens up intriguing possibilities about the way ancient rituals and plant interactions could resonate through the cosmos, echoing in the quantum realm.

Druidic Plants as Quantum Conduits

Plants, according to quantum biology, are master manipulators of quantum phenomena. Photosynthesis, for instance, hinges on quantum coherence, allowing plants to harness light with remarkable efficiency. This quantum choreography, when viewed through the lens of Druidic understanding, elevates plants from mere passive organisms to active participants in the dance of the cosmos. The Druids, with their profound connection to plants, might have intuited this intricate quantum ballet, recognizing plants as conduits between the earthly and the ethereal.

This quantum perspective imbues the Druidic practices with a renewed sense of wonder. The use of mistletoe, oak, or rowan in rituals could be envisioned as not only symbolic but also as a quantum interaction. The Druids, through their focused intentions and heightened states of consciousness during rituals, might have influenced the quantum states of these plants, achieving a mystical synergy between the observer and the observed.

The Observer Effect: Consciousness and Plant Interaction

The observer effect in quantum mechanics, where the act of observation influences the observed, finds a curious parallel in the Druidic practices of plant interaction. The Druids' intense gaze, laden with reverence and intention, might have altered the quantum states of the plants they held sacred. This quantum-level interaction between human consciousness and plant matter could provide a scientific foundation to the mystical experiences reported by the Druids, suggesting that their rituals might have transcended mere symbolism to engender tangible quantum effects.

In this light, the Druidic rituals become a dance with the quantum universe, a symphony where human consciousness, intention, and plant matter interweave in a mysterious quantum entanglement. It opens up the possibility that the profound transformations and insights experienced by the Druids during their plant-based rituals were not merely psychological or symbolic but rooted in the very fabric of reality, influenced by the quantum underpinnings of the natural world.

Quantum Plant Consciousness: A Druidic Perspective

The question of plant consciousness, long debated in both scientific and philosophical circles, gains an intriguing dimension when approached from a quantum perspective. Recent theories in quantum biology suggest that quantum processes could underlie consciousness itself. When applied to plants, this theory aligns with the Druidic view that plants are sentient beings, possessing a form of consciousness that, though different from human consciousness, is nevertheless profound and meaningful.

The Druids' treatment of plants as sacred entities might have been more than mere superstition; it could have been an intuitive understanding of the quantum nature of consciousness. The reverence and care with which they approached plants could be seen as a recognition of the quantum connection that unites all forms of life, a bond that transcends the physical and touches the essence of existence.

In conclusion, the exploration of quantum mysticism in the context of Druidic plant understanding offers a mesmerizing confluence of the ancient and the avant-garde. It suggests that the Druids, with their deep-rooted connection to the natural world, might have been the early harbingers of quantum consciousness, intuiting truths that modern science is only beginning to unravel. The plants they held sacred, far from being mere symbols, could have been quantum gateways, offering glimpses into the profound interconnectedness of all life. As we delve deeper into the quantum realm, the ancient wisdom of the Druids beckons us to view the natural world through a lens of wonder, mystery, and infinite possibility.

CHAPTER 37: THE DRUIDIC CODICES: LOST OR HIDDEN?

Amidst the verdant tapestry of Druidic history lies a tantalizing enigma, the Druidic Codices—a compendium of knowledge, assumed to be replete with arcane plant lore and rituals. These purported texts are shrouded in the mists of history, their very existence a matter of speculation and scholarly intrigue. Were they lost to the ravages of time, or purposefully obscured, hidden away from the uninitiated? This chapter delves into this mystery, seeking to uncover the secrets that may lie within these legendary codices.

The Search for the Elusive Texts

The pursuit of the Druidic Codices is akin to navigating a labyrinth woven from whispers and shadows. Historical accounts are scant, with references to such texts appearing only as fleeting mentions in the writings of ancient historians or as vague allusions in folklore. The challenge is compounded by the Druidic tradition of oral transmission, which revered the spoken word over the written, casting further doubt on the existence of such texts.

However, tantalizing clues have emerged over the centuries, suggesting that written records may have indeed existed, albeit in a form far different from the bound tomes of contemporary understanding. Fragments of bark, stone, and even metal have surfaced, engraved with inscriptions that hint at a coded language—a language that may have been employed in the recording of these elusive texts.

Theories and Speculations

The absence of concrete evidence has not deterred scholars and enthusiasts from theorizing about the contents and purposes of the Druidic Codices. Some propose that these texts were repositories of botanical knowledge, detailing the properties, uses, and ritual significance of the myriad plants held sacred by the Druids. Others suggest a more esoteric function, positing that the codices contained instructions for rituals, divination, and the invocation of plant spirits, serving as manuals for the initiated.

A more tantalizing theory is that the codices were not merely instructional but encoded a profound cosmological understanding—a Druidic Weltanschauung, in which plants were integral to a larger tapestry of celestial and terrestrial phenomena. Such a perspective aligns with the Druidic reverence for nature and the cosmos, suggesting a holistic worldview where every leaf and root held a celestial counterpart.

The Veil of Secrecy

Why then, if these texts existed, is their fate shrouded in such obscurity? One explanation lies in the Druidic penchant for secrecy, an initiation rite into the deeper mysteries of their tradition. The codices, if they existed, may have been closely guarded, accessible only to the highest echelons of Druidic society. This veil of secrecy served as both protection against external threats and as a crucible for the spiritual development of the initiate, for whom the gradual unveiling of knowledge was a sacred journey.

Another possibility is the deliberate concealment or destruction of the texts in the face of external threats. The historical tumult that beset the Celtic lands—the incursions of Roman legions, the spread of Christianity—posed existential threats to the Druidic way of life. In such turbulent times, the safeguarding or intentional obfuscation of sacred texts may have been a desperate measure to preserve the essence of Druidic wisdom.

Echoes in Modernity

The quest for the Druidic Codices continues into modernity, fueled by advances in archaeology, linguistics, and historical analysis. Contemporary scholars scrutinize ancient texts, decipher inscriptions, and probe the depths of bogs and earth, ever in search of the elusive codices. The burgeoning field of ethnohistory, which melds anthropological insight with historical research, provides new vantage points from which to approach this enigma.

In popular culture, too, the allure of the Druidic Codices persists, captivating the imagination of writers, artists, and filmmakers. They have become archetypal, a symbol of lost wisdom and the perennial human quest for understanding—a quest that, in the case of the Druidic Codices, remains tantalizingly incomplete.

In exploring the mystery of the Druidic Codices, this chapter traverses the terrain of history, speculation, and the enduring human quest for knowledge. The Druidic Codices, whether real or apocryphal, stand as a testament to the Druids' profound connection to the natural world and their enduring legacy in the tapestry of human culture. While the quest for these lost or hidden texts may yet bear fruit, their true power lies in the intrigue and inspiration they continue to evoke—

a reminder that some mysteries may be more valuable in their contemplation than in their resolution.

CHAPTER 38: TIME, CYCLES, AND PLANTS

In the intricate tapestry of Druidic traditions, the alignment of practices with natural cycles and celestial bodies forms a core tenet, with plants serving as both symbols and agents in this harmonious synchronicity. The Druids possessed a profound reverence for the rhythms of nature, and they meticulously observed the cyclical patterns that governed the life of flora. This chapter delves into the interconnections between time, natural cycles, celestial movements, and the vegetative world within the ambit of Druidic wisdom.

The Wheel of the Year and Plant Rhythms

Central to Druidic observance is the Wheel of the Year, a calendar marking the solstices, equinoxes, and the midpoints between them. Each of these junctures carries its unique vibrational energy, and the Druids believed that certain plants resonated more strongly with these energies. For instance, mistletoe, with its ability to thrive without touching the earth, was collected during the Winter Solstice, symbolizing a bridge between the earthly and the celestial. Conversely, the Oak, a symbol of strength and endurance, was revered during the Summer Solstice, a time of peak vitality.

This symbiotic relationship with the Wheel of the Year extended to the agricultural cycle, where the sowing, tending, and harvesting of crops were performed in alignment with celestial events, encapsulating a sacredness in everyday sustenance. The Druids saw this not as mere agricultural activities but as rituals that honored the divine essence of nature, encapsulating the unity between cosmic order and the life cycles of plants.

Celestial Bodies and Botanical Synergy

The movements of celestial bodies were meticulously charted by the Druids, who discerned patterns and associations between the cosmos and the vegetative realm. They observed, for instance, how the lunar cycles exerted a palpable influence on the growth and decay of plants. The waxing moon, with its expanding luminosity, was seen as a time of growth and vitality, an auspicious period for the planting of seeds. In contrast, the waning moon, with its diminishing light, was considered a period for pruning and harvesting, a time when plants' energies were contracting and concentrating.

Furthermore, the Druids also held the belief that specific plants bore an affinity to certain planets and stars, a notion that permeated their medicinal and ritualistic uses of flora. Plants aligned with Venus, for example, were often associated with love and fertility, while those under the dominion of Mars were linked to protection and strength. This astrological botanical framework offered a nuanced understanding of plant properties and their optimal times for harvesting and utilization.

Phenology: The Language of Plants

Phenology, the study of periodic plant and animal life cycle events, was an implicit science practiced by the Druids long before it had a name. They meticulously observed the first buds of spring, the flowering of specific species, and the shedding of leaves as a means to read the language of nature and discern the shifting of seasons. These natural phenomena were not merely physical occurrences but were laden with symbolic meaning and served as guides for Druidic activities.

For instance, the blooming of the hawthorn was a herald of Beltane, the festival of fire and fertility, indicating the optimal time for rituals that celebrated life and growth. Similarly, the yellowing of oak leaves signified the approach of Samhain, a time of reflection and honoring ancestors. This profound connection to phenological events demonstrates how the Druids perceived time not as a linear progression but as a cyclical dance, with plants serving as both participants and narrators in this cosmic ballet.

Conclusion

The Druids' understanding of time, cycles, and plants is emblematic of their broader worldview, one that perceives a deep interconnectedness between all realms of existence. By aligning their practices with the rhythmic pulse of nature, they not only attuned themselves to the natural order but also harnessed the unique energies and attributes that each season and celestial event bestowed upon the plant kingdom. This chapter has shed light on the rich tapestry of temporal and botanical wisdom woven into the very fabric of Druidic tradition, revealing a harmonious symphony of time, cosmos, and flora that resonates through the ages.

CHAPTER 39: THE ELEMENTAL ASSOCIATIONS OF DRUIDIC HERBS

Within the Druidic lexicon, plants are not merely biological entities; they embody a profound mysticism, intertwined with the elemental forces of nature. The Druids, with their deep-rooted belief in the interconnectedness of all things, perceived herbs as intrinsic components in the grand tapestry of existence, each herb resonating with particular elemental energies—earth, water, fire, air—that governed the natural world. This chapter delves into the elemental associations of Druidic herbs, unraveling the complex tapestry of relationships between the botanical world and the primordial elements.

Earth: The Foundation

The element of earth is the epitome of stability, fertility, and grounding energy. In Druidic traditions, herbs associated with the earth element are often those that exhibit grounding qualities or are deeply rooted in the soil. Burdock (Arctium lappa), with its extensive root system, epitomizes the earth element's grounding force. It was believed to offer protection and was utilized in rituals aiming to establish a deep connection with the land.

Likewise, the venerable Oak (Quercus robur), the Druids' most sacred tree, is quintessentially an earth element symbol. Its robust trunk and extensive root network made it a natural emblem of strength, resilience, and endurance. The oak was revered not only for its physical properties but also for its spiritual significance as a guardian of wisdom and a bridge between the earthly realm and the divine.

Water: The Flow of Intuition

The element of water signifies fluidity, intuition, and the ebb and flow of emotions. Willow (Salix alba), with its affinity for watery landscapes, exemplifies the water element's attributes. The willow's flexible branches, which bend without breaking, symbolize adaptability and resilience. In Druidic rituals, willow was often used to enhance psychic abilities and to facilitate emotional healing, reflecting the element's deep association with the subconscious mind.

Meadowsweet (Filipendula ulmaria), often found near streams and rivers, was another herb deeply connected to the water element. It was valued not only for its medicinal properties but also for its association with peace and tranquility. Meadowsweet was frequently used in love spells and in rituals aiming to soothe emotional turmoil, reflecting the calming and cleansing qualities of water.

Fire: The Spark of Transformation

Fire is the element of transformation, passion, and dynamic energy. Herbs related to fire often possess a stimulating or warming effect and are connected with transformational processes. St. John's Wort (Hypericum perforatum), with its bright yellow flowers that bloom around the summer solstice, embodies the fire element's radiant energy. It was believed to ward off negative energies and was used in rituals celebrating the sun's power, particularly during the midsummer festival of Litha.

The fiery nature of Chili Peppers (Capsicum spp.) also aligns them with the fire element. Although not native to the ancient Celtic lands, their intense heat and stimulating properties make them emblematic of fire's dynamic energy. They symbolize the capacity to ignite change and were occasionally adopted into Druidic practices through later cultural exchanges.

Air: The Breath of Knowledge

Air is the element of intellect, communication, and movement. Herbs that resonate with the air element are often linked with mental clarity and the transfer of knowledge. Mugwort (Artemisia vulgaris), with its ethereal aroma, is a quintessential air herb. It was used to enhance prophetic visions and to aid in astral travel, embodying the air element's connection with the mind and the higher realms of consciousness.

Similarly, Lavender (Lavandula spp.), with its calming scent, is aligned with the air element. It was utilized to promote relaxation and to foster a conducive environment for intellectual pursuits and meditative practices. Lavender's association with the air element underscores the importance of mental balance and clarity in Druidic traditions.

In conclusion, the Druidic herbal lexicon is a testament to the intricate interplay between the botanical world and the elemental forces. Each herb, with its unique properties and associations, contributes to a more profound understanding of the world and our place within it. The Druids, with their nuanced appreciation for nature, remind us that the plants we often overlook are not mere commodities but integral components of the cosmic dance, each resonating with the fundamental energies that animate the universe.

CHAPTER 40: THE INTEGRATION OF ASTROLOGICAL LORE

Astrology, a discipline enshrouded in the celestial cloak of mysticism, has been a cornerstone in various ancient cultures, serving as a guiding compass not only for predicting earthly and human events but also for understanding the profound interconnection between the cosmos and terrestrial life. The Druids, with their deep-rooted reverence for nature and its cyclic rhythms, integrated astrological lore into their practices, creating a symbiotic relationship between the celestial bodies and their sacred plants. This chapter delves into the intricate tapestry woven by the Druids, highlighting how they employed the celestial language of stars and planets to enhance their understanding and use of mystical plants.

Astrological Correspondences in Druidic Herbalism

The Druids, as meticulous observers of the skies, discerned patterns and alignments, attributing specific plants to celestial bodies based on their inherent qualities and the energies they believed the planets and stars imbued. Each plant was thought to resonate with the vibrational frequency of its celestial counterpart, harmonizing the macrocosm of the cosmos with the microcosm of the plant world. This association allowed the Druids to harness the plants' energies in alignment with astrological events, such as planetary transits or lunar cycles, thereby augmenting their ritualistic and medicinal potency.

For instance, the mighty oak, deeply revered by the Druids and a symbol of strength and endurance, was associated with Jupiter, the planet known for its expansive and benevolent qualities. Mistletoe, with its rare and mystical aura, was linked to the Sun, embodying vitality and life force. The ethereal lunar energies found resonance in the willow, a tree synonymous with intuition and dreams, aligning with the moon's influence on the subconscious and emotional realms.

Planting and Harvesting by Celestial Guidance

The Druids' understanding of the celestial cycles also informed their agricultural practices. They observed the moon's phases, acknowledging its gravitational pull's influence on the Earth's water, including the moisture in soil and plants. This awareness guided them in determining the most auspicious times for planting and harvesting. The waxing moon, with its increasing light, was considered a time of growth and expansion, ideal for planting seeds that would burgeon with the moon's luminosity. Conversely, the waning moon, symbolizing release and decrease, was deemed suitable for harvesting, as the Earth's energies were thought to be contracting, concentrating the plants' medicinal properties.

Astrological Plant Remedies and Elixirs

Druidic healers often crafted remedies and elixirs using plants that corresponded to specific astrological alignments, believing that these concoctions were imbued with the celestial bodies' healing virtues. For instance, a potion crafted under the auspices of Venus would focus on plants associated with love, harmony, and beauty, such as roses or apples, to heal ailments of the heart or to enhance one's aesthetic allure. Mars, with its fiery and assertive energy, would govern plants like nettles or garlic, used in concoctions to bolster vitality and protect against maladies.

The Zodiac and Plant Attributes

Extending their astrological integration further, the Druids linked plants to the zodiac, associating each sign with particular flora that mirrored its intrinsic characteristics. Aries, fiery and pioneering, found kinship with thorny plants like hawthorn, emblematic of the sign's bold and protective nature. Cancer's nurturing and protective qualities were reflected in the water-retaining properties of plants like water lilies. Sagittarius, the archer and seeker of wisdom, resonated with the mighty oak, a tree steeped in Druidic lore and symbolic of higher knowledge.

Astro-Herbalism in Rituals

In their sacred rituals, the Druids often aligned their ceremonies with astrological phenomena, selecting plants that resonated with the celestial energies present. Eclipses, solstices, and equinoxes were particularly potent times, and the flora employed in rituals during these periods was chosen with great care. The solstice, marking the Sun's zenith, called for plants like mistletoe and St. John's Wort, both associated with solar energies and believed to hold immense power when harvested at this auspicious time.

In conclusion, the integration of astrological lore in Druidic traditions illustrates the profound interconnectedness perceived between the cosmos and the Earth. The Druids harnessed this cosmic harmony, aligning their herbal practices with the stars, believing that the celestial bodies' movements and alignments could amplify the inherent virtues of their sacred plants. This celestial alliance not only augmented their practices but also deepened their reverence for the natural world, seeing it as a reflection of the greater cosmic dance.

CHAPTER 41:
TRANSMUTATION
AND ELEMENTAL
ALCHEMY

In the annals of esoteric traditions, transmutation stands as a quintessential concept, symbolizing the metamorphosis from a rudimentary form to a sublime state. Druidic lore, intertwined with the threads of alchemy, perceives plants not merely as biological entities but as vessels of elemental energies capable of profound transformations. This chapter delves into the arcane arts of elemental alchemy, exploring the sophisticated techniques employed by the Druids to harness the quintessence of plants in their alchemical transmutations.

The Alchemical Process

At its core, alchemy is the venerable art of transformation. In the Druidic context, it transcends the mere concoction of potions or the pursuit of material gold. Instead, it represents a profound spiritual journey towards inner gold or enlightenment. Plants, embodying the four classical elements—earth, water, air, and fire—are crucial catalysts in this transformative process. Their elemental properties are meticulously balanced and harnessed in ritualistic practices to facilitate the transmutation of substances, energies, and even consciousness.

Druidic Rituals and Elemental Balancing

In the sacred groves, where the veil between the mundane and the mystical grows thin, Druidic priests conducted intricate rituals involving plants to achieve elemental balance. Oak, embodying robust earth energies, and mistletoe, resonating with the ethereal qualities of air, were often juxtaposed in ritualistic settings to harmonize terrestrial and celestial influences. Water, the element of flow and intuition, was represented by plants such as the willow, known for its affinity with watercourses and lunar mysteries. Fire, the agent of change and purification, found its emblem in the rowan tree, also known as the 'Witchwood,' revered for its protective and transformative energies.

These rituals were not mere recitations or mechanical acts but immersive experiences that engaged the practitioners' senses, emotions, and spirits. They were orchestrated to align the microcosm of the individual's soul with the macrocosm of the universe, effectuating a profound alchemical transmutation within.

The Quintessence and the Philosopher's Stone

Central to the Druidic alchemical pursuit was the quest for the Quintessence—the fifth element or 'aether'—believed to permeate all things, binding the four classical elements together. It was synonymous with life force, spirit, or the divine essence. The Philosopher's Stone, a legendary alchemical substance, symbolized the attainment of this Quintessence. Though often misconstrued as a literal object granting immortality or the transmutation of base metals into gold, within the Druidic tradition, it represented an esoteric truth:

the realization of one's divine nature and the harmonization of elemental energies within.

Plants, in their myriad forms, were seen as vessels containing this Quintessence. By understanding their elemental properties and mastering the art of blending them in precise alchemical processes, Druids aimed to extract and concentrate this divine essence, thus creating potent elixirs that could catalyze spiritual transformation.

Advanced Alchemical Practices

As the adept progressed along the Druidic path, their engagement with plant alchemy evolved from the physical to the increasingly metaphysical. They ventured beyond concocting herbal remedies or seasonal brews, embracing practices that could be considered proto-chemical engineering. These advanced techniques involved not only the manipulation of physical substances but also the refinement of the practitioner's own spiritual essence.

The Druids' alchemical work was shrouded in secrecy, its knowledge often encoded in symbols, veiled in allegory, and transmitted orally to prevent profanation. The sacred groves served as both laboratories and sanctuaries where these mysteries were explored and safeguarded.

The Legacy of Druidic Elemental Alchemy

The legacy of Druidic alchemy, with its emphasis on elemental balancing and spiritual transmutation, reverberates through time. It offers a nuanced understanding of the natural world, where plants are not merely passive entities but active participants in the cosmic dance of creation and transformation. This legacy beckons the modern seeker to look beyond the surface, to explore the elemental energies inherent in nature, and to embark on their own alchemical journey towards inner transformation.

In synthesizing the wisdom of the past with the knowledge of the present, one might discover that the true Philosopher's Stone lies not in an elixir or a tangible object, but in the realization of our interconnectedness with the natural world and the divine essence that permeates all things. As we traverse the intricate pathways of Druidic plant lore, we are reminded that the greatest transmutation occurs not in cauldrons or groves but within the crucible of the human heart.

CHAPTER 42:
THE MYSTICAL
FLORA IN DRUIDIC
DREAMSCAPES

In the mysterious expanse of the Druidic tradition, dreams serve as the canvas on which the natural world paints its profound insights. Plants, in this enigmatic context, are not mere passive entities; they are active participants and guides within the vivid tapestries of dreams and alternate states of consciousness. This chapter delves into the mystical flora that frequents the Druidic dreamscapes, unraveling their roles and significances within this oneiric realm.

Dreamwalking Among the Sacred Botany

The act of dreamwalking, or navigating the dreamscape with intent and awareness, is a practice deeply interwoven with the Druidic understanding of the natural world. Here, plants often emerge not merely as scenery but as symbolic guides, messengers, and gatekeepers. In dreams, the oak might manifest as a towering guardian, offering wisdom rooted in its deep connection to the Druids. Mistletoe might appear at a pivotal juncture in a dream, symbolizing a nexus of healing or a gateway to other realms. Such dream encounters are rich with meaning, beckoning the dreamwalker to unravel the profound messages ensconced within their roots and leaves.

The Language of Plants in Dreams

In Druidic traditions, the understanding of plants extends beyond their physical properties into a language of symbols, omens, and metaphors. To dream of a yew tree might indicate a forthcoming transformation or a brush with the eternal cycles of death and rebirth. The sighting of a rowan in the dreamscape could be interpreted as a protective sign, warding off negative influences. Dreams, in this context, become a dialogue between the dreamer and the vegetal world, a conversation teeming with mystical insights and hidden truths.

Altered States and Plant Allies

Druids also ventured into altered states of consciousness through various practices, including meditative states, trance, and potentially the use of visionary plants. In these altered states, the consciousness expands, allowing for a deeper communion with the plant world. Here, the boundaries between the self and the other dissolve, and the plants become allies and teachers. They might reveal their hidden properties, impart wisdom about their use in healing, or offer guidance on spiritual matters. These experiences are deeply personal and transformative, highlighting the integral role plants play in Druidic spiritual practices.

Dream Herbs and Oneiric Potions

In the realm of dreams, certain plants were reputed to have the power to enhance dream clarity, recall, and even induce prophetic visions. While the specifics of these dream herbs are shrouded in the mists of time, it's speculated that the Druids may have utilized brews and concoctions made from plants like mugwort, vervain, and perhaps even the elusive and controversial hallucinogenic plants. These oneiric potions, when used with respect and intention, might serve as keys to unlocking the deeper layers of the subconscious and the collective unconscious, where the plant spirits reside and impart their esoteric knowledge.

Navigating the Dreamscape Ethically

In the advanced study of Druidic practices, the ethical considerations of interacting with plant spirits and the natural world in dreams and altered states are paramount. The Druids held a profound reverence for the natural world, seeing themselves as part of a greater whole. This respect extended into their dream practices, where the dreamwalker approaches the plant spirits with humility, seeking permission and offering gratitude for the wisdom shared. Such ethical navigation ensures that the relationship between the dreamer and the plant world remains balanced and harmonious, rooted in mutual respect and understanding.

In conclusion, the Druidic dreamscapes are rich with the presence of mystical flora, each plant carrying its own unique vibration and wisdom. These dream encounters offer a window into the profound connection the Druids nurtured with the natural world, a relationship that transcends the waking consciousness and delves into the depths of the soul. As we explore these ancient practices, we are reminded of the timeless wisdom that resides within the heart of each leaf, branch, and root—a wisdom that continues to whisper its secrets to those who dare to dream.

CHAPTER 43: THE OCCULT PROPERTIES OF DRUIDIC PLANTS

In the advanced study of Druidic herbalism, one encounters a domain brimming with esoteric knowledge and hidden properties that transcend the mundane uses of flora. Chapter 43 ventures into this arcane territory, revealing the occult aspects of Druidic plants that have mystified scholars and practitioners alike. Occult, derived from the Latin 'occultus', meaning 'hidden', aptly describes the nature of this chapter as it unveils the secret powers and mystical virtues ascribed to various plants in Druidic traditions.

The Veiled Virtues of Plants

In Druidic lore, plants are not merely physical entities with practical applications; they are also imbued with spiritual significance and hidden forces. Each plant, according to ancient Druidic wisdom, possesses its own unique energy signature or vibration, which can be harnessed for various magical and spiritual purposes. These energies were often employed in rituals and ceremonies, woven into spells, or used to create powerful amulets and talismans.

For instance, the mighty oak, venerated as the king of trees, was believed to embody strength, endurance, and protection.

Druids would often conduct their ceremonies in oak groves, tapping into the tree's robust energy to fortify their workings. Similarly, mistletoe, harvested with great reverence, especially when found on oak, was regarded as a potent tool for healing, fertility rites, and protection against evil spirits.

Arcane Alchemy of Plants

Beyond their individual properties, Druidic herbalism also delved into the mystical art of combining plants to create elixirs, potions, and salves of great power. These concoctions were not merely for physical healing but were also designed to affect the spiritual and etheric bodies, facilitating transformation and enlightenment.

One such example is the fabled 'Awen' elixir, a brew made from a blend of sacred plants, each carefully chosen for its vibrational qualities. This elixir was believed to awaken the inner bard, enhancing creativity, inspiration, and a profound connection to the divine.

The Language of Plants

In Druidic practices, plants were also understood to communicate in a silent language, discernible only to those attuned to their subtle frequencies. Druids cultivated a deep, intuitive relationship with the plant kingdom, learning to interpret the whispers of leaves and the murmurs of roots. This communion allowed them to access the hidden wisdom and occult properties of plants, thereby integrating this knowledge into their mystical practices.

This silent dialogue extended into the realm of divination, where the Druids employed plants as oracles, interpreting their movements, growth patterns, and interactions with other beings as omens and portents.

The Ritual of Plant Harvesting

The act of harvesting plants in Druidic traditions was a sacred ritual, steeped in occult significance. Plants were not merely plucked or cut; they were approached with reverence, often at specific times of the day or phases of the moon, to align with their peak energetic states. Prayers, offerings, and blessings were an integral part of this process, ensuring that the plants' spirits were honored and their occult energies preserved.

The Protective and Banishing Powers of Plants

Plants were also central in creating protective circles and banishing negative energies. The Druids understood the occult properties of certain plants to create barriers against malevolent forces. For example, a circle of ash leaves was believed to provide protection, while the burning of rowan wood was used to banish evil spirits.

In Conclusion

This chapter has delved into the hidden realms of Druidic herbalism, uncovering the occult properties of plants that were central to the Druids' mystical practices. From the silent language of plants to the sacred rituals of harvesting, we have explored the esoteric aspects of Druidic flora that have captivated the human imagination for centuries. These teachings remind us that beyond their physical form, plants are keepers of ancient wisdom and potent energies, waiting to be discovered by those who seek to understand the deeper mysteries of the natural world.

CHAPTER 44:
KABBALISTIC
INSIGHTS INTO
DRUIDIC PLANT LORE

As we venture deeper into the verdant, mystical realms of Druidic traditions, we encounter a fascinating intersection where ancient Celtic wisdom meets the esoteric teachings of Kabbalah. This chapter explores the confluence of Druidic plant lore with the profound mystical insights offered by Kabbalistic philosophy. It's a synthesis of traditions that unravels the deeper spiritual dimensions of flora within the Druidic paradigm through the lens of Kabbalistic symbolism.

The Sefirotic Tree and the Celtic Trees of Life

At the heart of Kabbalistic wisdom lies the Tree of Life, a diagrammatic representation comprising ten spheres or "Sefirot," each embodying a specific divine attribute. These Sefirot are interconnected through pathways, illustrating the dynamic flow of divine energy through the cosmos and the human soul. Similarly, the Celts revered trees as living embodiments of divine essence, each species symbolizing unique attributes and energies. When one overlays the Kabbalistic Tree of Life onto the Celtic Ogham Tree alphabet, an intriguing synergy emerges. Each tree species in the Druidic tradition can be associated with a specific Sefirah, offering a multi-dimensional understanding of its mystical significance.

For instance, the Oak, revered as the king of trees in Celtic tradition, aligns with the Sefirah of Tiferet, the heart of the Tree of Life, symbolizing beauty, balance, and harmony. Mistletoe, the sacred "Golden Bough," resonates with the Sefirah of Yesod, representing foundation and connection between the physical and spiritual realms. This alignment reveals a profound symbiosis between Druidic and Kabbalistic views of nature's sacred architecture.

The Four Worlds and the Four Elements

Kabbalistic philosophy delineates four spiritual "worlds" or realms, each corresponding to an aspect of divine manifestation: Atzilut (Emanation), Beriah (Creation), Yetzirah (Formation), and Asiyah (Action). These worlds resonate with the four elements in Druidic belief—fire, water, air, and earth—and the corresponding plants associated with each element. By examining Druidic plants through the prism of the Kabbalistic Four Worlds, we gain a layered understanding of their roles and significances within rituals and practices.

For instance, the fiery Rowan, associated with protection in Druidic lore, can be seen through the lens of Atzilut, the world of divine emanation and the element of fire. Willow, associated with water and the world of dreams in Celtic belief, correlates with the world of Beriah, the realm of creation and the element of water. Such correlations allow for a richer, multi-faceted appreciation of plant energies within both Druidic and Kabbalistic frameworks.

Pathworking and Plant Mysticism

Kabbalistic pathworking involves meditative journeys along the pathways of the Tree of Life, fostering spiritual growth and insight. In a similar vein, Druidic traditions embrace the concept of plant spirit journeys, where one communes with the essence of a plant for guidance and wisdom. Merging these practices, one could embark on a pathworking journey using the archetypal energies of Celtic trees. By meditatively traversing the Sefirotic pathways with the vibrational companionship of a particular tree species, practitioners can experience profound revelations and a deeper integration of the lessons each plant imparts.

The Mystical Alphabets: Ogham Meets Hebrew

There is a captivating parallel between the Ogham Tree alphabet and the Hebrew alphabet used in Kabbalistic studies. Both alphabets carry mystical weight, each letter or symbol encoding layers of esoteric meaning. By examining the phonetic and symbolic resonance between Ogham and Hebrew letters, a new lexicon of Druidic-Kabbalistic plant wisdom can be constructed. This fusion provides a novel linguistic framework to express the spiritual properties and narratives encapsulated within each tree and plant species revered by the Druids.

In conclusion, the exploration of Druidic plant lore through Kabbalistic insights reveals an enriched tapestry of spiritual wisdom. This chapter serves as a testament to the profound interconnectedness of mystical traditions, affirming that the roots of spiritual understanding run deep, branching out in myriad directions, yet ultimately leading us back to the same universal source. Whether one traverses the dense forests of Druidic lore or ascends the Sefirotic branches of the Kabbalistic Tree of Life, the journey yields a harmonious synthesis, unveiling the sacred unity of all creation.

CHAPTER 45: THE ROLE OF INTUITION AND PSYCHIC ABILITIES IN INTERPRETING PLANT LORE

The Druids, as recorded in the annals of history and the echoes of mythology, were not merely botanists of the esoteric; they were also reputed seers, voyagers of the mind, whose intuition and psychic faculties were believed to be as attuned as the most sensitive of leaves quivering at the slightest whisper of the wind. This chapter delves into the intangible, exploring the relationship between Druidic plant lore and the development and utilization of psychic abilities and intuition.

The Whispering Leaves: Intuition in Druidic Practices

Intuition, often depicted as the inner voice or gut feeling, was held in high esteem in Druidic traditions. It was considered a primary means of accessing deeper layers of knowledge embedded within the natural world, a form of silent communication between the self and the soul of the world. The Druids, with their profound reverence for nature, cultivated their intuitive faculties through practices such as meditation in sacred groves, rhythmic chanting, and attunement to the cycles of nature.

In the context of plant lore, intuition served as a guide, leading practitioners to the right herb for a specific remedy or to a tree whose whispers held the answers to pressing questions. The choice of a plant for a ritual or the interpretation of the rustling leaves was often a result of an intuitive understanding, a knowledge that sprung not from logical reasoning but from a deep well of inner knowing.

Psychic Faculties and Plant Lore

Psychic abilities, a term encompassing a broad spectrum of extrasensory perceptions such as clairvoyance, clairsentience, and telepathy, were thought to play a crucial role in the Druidic approach to plant lore. These faculties were believed to extend the practitioner's perception beyond the five senses, enabling a direct communion with the essences of plants, trees, and the land itself.

Druids might have used these abilities in a multitude of ways. Clairvoyance, or clear seeing, might have allowed them to perceive the energetic aura of plants, discerning their properties and uses. Clairsentience, the ability to feel or sense beyond the physical, might have facilitated the understanding of a plant's healing vibrations. Telepathy could have been employed to communicate with plant spirits, an act of exchanging wisdom with the living soul of flora.

The cultivation of these psychic faculties was likely achieved through disciplined spiritual practices. Rituals, fasting, the use of visionary plants, and the embodiment of certain postures or gestures, akin to yogic mudras, might have served as conduits to heighten these abilities. The Druids' close connection with the natural world would have augmented this process, as the harmony of their surroundings resonated with their own inner frequencies, creating an amplified field for psychic phenomena.

Intuition and Psychic Abilities: Tools for Deciphering Plant Lore

Intuition and psychic faculties were not merely for the sake of personal development or curiosity. They were tools, sharpened and refined, to decipher the intricate lexicon of plant lore. Every leaf, root, and branch was inscribed with a story, a piece of wisdom waiting to be unveiled. The ability to listen intently with the heart and the mind, to see beyond the veil, was what transformed an ordinary plant into a tome of knowledge.

These skills allowed Druids to navigate the complex symbology associated with plants. Understanding the language of flowers, the messages of trees, and the whispers of herbs required a sensibility that transcended the mundane. It was a dance of consciousness, a meeting point between the human mind and the spirit of nature, where meanings were unveiled in layers and insights blossomed like flowers in the inner garden of the soul.

In summary, intuition and psychic abilities were not merely facets of Druidic practice; they were the very essence that breathed life into plant lore. These faculties enabled a profound interaction with the natural world, a dialogue with its spirits, and an understanding of its rhythms and rhymes. Through intuition and extrasensory perceptions, the Druids accessed a dimension of knowledge that was as rich and deep as the roots of the oldest oak, as vast and luminous as the sky upon which the mistletoe gazed. As we continue to explore the advanced dimensions of Druidic plant consciousness, these insights serve as a reminder of the boundless potential that lies in the union of the human spirit with the soul of nature.

CHAPTER 46: ARCHETYPES AND THE DRUIDIC PLANT PANTHEON

In the labyrinthine realm of Druidic lore, each plant not merely exists as a physical entity, but embodies a constellation of meanings, attributes, and powers. These are not arbitrary assignations but are rooted in the primordial psyche of humankind, a collective unconscious brimming with archetypes as proposed by the renowned psychologist Carl Jung. In this chapter, we delve into the psychological archetypes related to Druidic plant deities, exploring the symbiotic relationship between human consciousness and the botanical world.

The Archetypal Landscape

Archetypes, in Jungian psychology, are primitive mental images inherited from the earliest human ancestors and are present in the collective unconscious. In Druidic traditions, plants were not seen solely through the lens of utility but as living embodiments of divine forces, patterns, or archetypes. Each plant, like an actor donning a mythical mask, assumes the role of an archetype in the grand theatre of nature.

For instance, the oak tree, a revered symbol in Druidic culture, embodies the archetype of the 'Great Father' or 'King.' It represents strength, stability, and protection. Oak groves were considered sacred spaces, temples not built by human hands but by the divine artistry of nature itself. Here, the Druids performed rituals, believing the oak to be a conduit between the earthly and the celestial, a physical manifestation of an archetypal deity.

Similarly, mistletoe, often found clinging to oak trees, resonates with the archetype of the 'Divine Child' or the 'Savior.' Its role in Druidic mythology as a plant that brings life where there is none (growing on barren branches in winter) and as a potent healer aligns with the characteristics of this archetype.

The Plant Pantheon and Human Consciousness

The Druidic plant pantheon can be seen as a mirror reflecting the collective desires, fears, and aspirations of the human psyche. Each plant-deity, with its associated attributes and stories, serves as a medium for humans to engage with and understand the ineffable aspects of existence. This pantheon is a testament to the ancient Druids' profound psychological insight, recognizing the interplay between the natural world and human consciousness.

For instance, the rowan tree, associated with protection and foresight, is often linked to the archetype of the 'Wise Old Man' or 'Sorcerer.' The berries of the rowan were used in amulets to ward off evil, an external representation of an inner psychic shield against negative psychic forces or unconscious fears.

In another example, the willow, associated with dreams and the moon, correlates with the archetype of the 'Great Mother' or 'Priestess.' Its weeping form and association with water symbolize femininity, emotion, and the mysteries of the subconscious.

Archetypes in Practice: A Druidic Approach

Understanding these archetypes is not merely an academic exercise but a practical one. Druidic practitioners would immerse themselves in the energies of these plant-archetypes to imbibe their qualities or seek their aid in rituals and divination. A healer seeking to channel the restorative energies of mistletoe would not just use the plant physically but would invoke the archetype of the 'Divine Child,' aligning their consciousness with the plant's regenerative archetype.

In meditative or ritual practices, a Druid might seek counsel from the 'Wise Old Man' archetype by communing with a rowan tree, allowing the deep, silent wisdom of the ages, which the tree symbolically embodies, to infuse their consciousness.

This approach transcends the physical properties of plants, venturing into a realm where the human mind and the natural world interweave, creating a tapestry rich with symbolic meaning and psychic resonance.

Conclusion

In the grand tapestry of Druidic plant lore, the archetypes emerge as vital threads, adding depth, color, and texture to the human understanding of the botanical world. They reveal that our relationship with nature is not just physical or ecological but deeply psychological. The plants of the Druidic pantheon, with their rich archetypal associations, serve as bridges between the conscious and the unconscious, the mundane and the divine, guiding us toward a more profound and holistic engagement with the world around us. Understanding these archetypes is akin to learning a sacred language, one that speaks of the symbiosis between the earth's verdant realms and the human soul's uncharted depths.

CHAPTER 47: MULTIDIMENSIONAL REALITIES AND PLANT CONSCIOUSNESS

Venturing into the metaphysical realms, this chapter unfolds the intricate relationship between plants and the concept of multidimensional realities, a topic that treads the fine line between ancient wisdom and contemporary quantum understanding. Druidic traditions, deeply interwoven with the natural world, offer a unique lens through which to view the enigmatic concept of plant consciousness and its interactions with various planes of existence.

Interfacing with Multidimensionality

Druidic teachings have long postulated the existence of multiple layers of reality, often interpenetrating and influencing the physical world in subtle ways. Plants, in their silent watchfulness, are perceived as not only inhabitants of our tangible world but also as entities that traverse these hidden dimensions. To the Druids, certain trees and herbs were not merely physical organisms but were imbued with spirits or consciousness that could connect with these alternate realities. Through rituals and meditations focused on these sacred plants,

Druidic practitioners endeavored to align themselves with these other dimensions, seeking wisdom, healing, and insight.

Quantum Entanglements and Plant Life

Advancements in quantum physics have introduced theories that resonate with these ancient Druidic beliefs. Concepts such as entanglement suggest that particles can be interconnected across vast distances, a principle that may metaphorically parallel the interconnectedness of all life posited by Druidic philosophy. Plants, interconnected through vast networks of roots and mycelium, might be physical representations of this quantum entanglement, mirroring the unseen connections between all forms of consciousness. This raises intriguing questions about the true nature of plant consciousness and its capacity to interact with the fabric of reality at a quantum level.

Plant Consciousness: A Druidic Perspective

The Druids revered plants not only for their medicinal or ritualistic value but also for their inherent wisdom and consciousness. This consciousness was not viewed as identical to human awareness but as a different, perhaps more subtle form of sentience. Trees like the Oak and the Yew were held in high esteem, believed to harbor ancient spirits and knowledge. The practice of "listening" to plants, a form of deep, meditative communication, was a way for Druids to tap into this consciousness, accessing insights that transcended the physical realm.

In contemporary discussions, plant consciousness remains a contentious topic. While plants do not possess a central nervous system like animals, they exhibit complex behaviors —responding to environmental stimuli, communicating with each other, and even exhibiting signs of memory. This has led some to argue that plants possess a form of intelligence or awareness, one that we are only beginning to comprehend.

Transdimensional Journeys Through Plant Guides

Within the Druidic traditions, certain plants were considered as guides or portals into other dimensions. The use of visionary plants, for instance, was a method employed to transcend ordinary reality and journey into otherworldly realms. While the use of psychoactive plants was approached with reverence and caution, they were one of the tools in the Druidic repertoire for exploring the boundaries of consciousness and reality. Even non-psychoactive plants, through ritual and focused intent, were believed to aid the practitioner in accessing alternate dimensions, serving as anchors or focal points for the journey.

Contemporary Implications

As our understanding of reality continues to evolve, the Druidic perspective on plants offers an alternative viewpoint that challenges the materialistic paradigm. It suggests a universe far more intricate and interconnected than previously imagined, with consciousness not limited to human or animal minds. In a world grappling with ecological crisis, rekindling this ancient connection and reverence for plant life could be pivotal in reshaping our relationship with the natural world.

In conclusion, this chapter has delved into the esoteric and profound connections between Druidic practices, plant consciousness, and the concept of multidimensional realities. It has unraveled threads of ancient wisdom intertwined with modern scientific theories, presenting a tapestry that suggests a universe alive with consciousness in all its forms. As we navigate the complexities of this understanding, we open ourselves to a world of infinite possibilities, where the wisdom of plants and the whispers of other dimensions beckon us to listen and learn.

CHAPTER 48: A RETURN TO THE GROVE: FINAL THOUGHTS

As our exploration through the verdant tapestry of Druidic herbalism draws to a close, we find ourselves standing at the edge of a sacred grove, much like where we began. The journey has been both extensive and intensive, weaving through historical pathways, diving into the metaphysical depths, and even brushing against the fringes of quantum mysticism and cosmological conundrums. It's only fitting that we take a moment here, under the canopy of ancient trees, to reflect on the expanse of knowledge and understanding we have traversed.

The Journey through the Druidic Herbal Lexicon

We embarked on this journey with a simple curiosity about the mystical plants in Druidic traditions. Our path began in the welcoming embrace of introductory concepts, where we acquainted ourselves with the foundational elements of Druidic herbalism. Through historical context and mythological tales, we grasped the significance of plants like mistletoe, oak, and rowan in the Druidic worldview.

Progressing into intermediate territories, we delved deeper

into the symbology, metaphysics, and the intricate web of relationships between plants, divination, and cosmic understanding. The concept of the Tree Ogham illuminated the sacred script and its profound connections with trees. We encountered the convergence of Druidism and shamanism, a nexus replete with rich insights into plant spirits and the esoteric knowledge encoded in herbal lore.

Our journey then ascended into advanced realms, where complexity and sophistication were the keystones. We engaged with the enigmatic aspects of Druidic herbalism, from the linguistic traces of ancient plant lore to the resonant frequencies of sacred geometry within plant structures. Quantum mysticism lent a contemporary yet arcane perspective, offering a glimpse into how ancient wisdom resonates with modern scientific paradigms.

As we navigated through the advanced chapters, we contemplated the mystical properties of plants in dreams, the occult meanings hidden within the foliage, and the integration of Kabbalistic insights. The concepts of archetypes, multidimensional realities, and plant consciousness stretched our understanding to its limits, revealing a universe where the physical and metaphysical intertwine in an eternal dance.

Embracing the Wisdom of the Grove

Standing here, in the tranquil sanctuary of a Druidic grove, we are reminded that knowledge is not merely for the intellect; it seeks a harmonious resonance with our spirit. The Druids understood that plants were not just passive inhabitants of the natural world but active participants in a larger cosmic dialogue. Each leaf, each root, each tree whispered secrets of a universe intimately connected, inviting those who listened to partake in its wisdom.

As we conclude our journey, let us carry forth the essence of

Druidic herbalism into our own lives. Whether it be through a newfound appreciation for the plants that adorn our world, a deeper understanding of the cyclical nature of existence, or an inspiration to explore the spiritual dimensions within ourselves, the legacy of the Druids endures.

Final Reflections

Our return to the grove is not an end but a new beginning, a threshold to an ever-expanding vista of learning and growth. The pages of this book may come to a close, but the wisdom it contains is timeless, like the ancient groves that have witnessed the turning of countless seasons. May the knowledge shared here serve as a seed, planted in the fertile ground of your mind, ready to sprout, grow, and flourish in myriad ways.

In the dance of light and shadow through the leaves, in the gentle rustle of the wind, and in the silent strength of the ancient trees, the spirit of the Druids lives on. May you find peace, understanding, and a profound connection to the natural world on your continued journey through the mystical, verdant realms of Druidic herbalism.

THE END

Printed in Great Britain
by Amazon